Far As I Can Remember

"Minnie Rose Enefer/Lovgreen's life story, told in her down-to-earth style, is an amazing tale of a Victorian girl's journey from a small English village to life in the New World….heartwarming…beautiful….will leave readers feeling they have made a new friend in Minnie Rose."
   ~Pam Griffin, *North Shropshire Chronicle*, **UK**

"Reading this book is more than reading words. It's like hearing a voice in your ear and mind that remains long after the pages end….Minnie Rose lives in these pages with all her homespun wit, courage and wisdom."
   ~Bob McAllister, Professor of English, Olympic College, WA

"….astonishing detail….extraordinary storytelling gifts. For Minnie Rose Lovgreen, 'far as I can remember' is a very long way indeed."
   ~Kathleen Thorne, Adult Program Coord., Kitsap Regional Library, WA

"It is one thing researching ancestors from censuses and certificates, but quite another to hear their stories direct. Minnie Rose Enefer/Lovgreen is sadly no longer with us….she has left us a story of a poor country girl who through sheer determination made something of her life….in her own words, the book brings to life an incredible woman who can only be described as a unique character, perhaps the sort of character that sadly no longer exists. She understates both her hardships and achievements, but her quick fire mind and quaint turn of phrase make her story both engaging and inspirational…. makes me proud of my surname–I just only wish I can live up to it."
   ~Andy Enefer, distant relative of Minnie Rose, Verwood, Dorset, UK

"Part *Giants in the Earth* and part *Foxfire Book*….I am in awe of her genius for memory, storytelling, practicality and good humor."
   ~Mary Gleystein, Eagle Harbor Book Co., Bainbridge Island, WA

"…a woman of incredible strength and determination….intriguing and engrossing…..could not put it down…."
~**Hank Helm, Dir., Bainbridge Isl. Historical Museum, Bainbridge Isl., WA**

"A few pages into (this book) I stopped seeing the words on the page. It was as if Minnie Rose was speaking directly to me. Her humor, wisdom, and unique life experience kept me enchanted for hours....and her thoughts have stayed with me."
   ~Trude Lisagor, author of *Small Things: Words from my namesake*

"....testament to what good health and a strong back could earn a British immigrant in 1915...." **~Kathleen Alcala, author of** *Treasures in Heaven*

"Warm, funny, and wise....Minnie Rose Lovgreen's story is the story of the American immigrant experience....bringing such rich history to the printed page." **~Rebecca Judd, Branch Manager, Bainbridge Public Library**

"If you enjoy the history of 'ordinary' people's lives....you'll love the story of Minnie Rose Lovgreen...."
   ~Linda Carlson, author of *Company Towns of the Pacific Northwest*

"....rare chronicle of an immigrant's life from a woman's perspective."
   ~Connie Mears, *Bainbridge Island Review*

Recipe for Raising Chickens, now in 3rd edition

"....finely crafted book....charming in its presentation and knowledgeable in its scope...."
   ~Thornton McEnery, Asst. Editor, *Country Living Magazine, May 2010*

"splendid guide for beginners and an absolute delight for chicken lovers everywhere....explains that chickens are the gardner's best friends, eagerly eating weeds, seeds and bugs. They fluff up the soil beautifully, enriching it with their homemade fertilizer...."
   Ann Lovejoy, author/educator/chicken lover

"....I love Minnie Rose's observations, many....very familiar...Also many, completely new, explain behaviours I never took the trouble to understand or analyze....Also she explains why we look after our own chickens in certain ways–ways I never questioned....was never told the reasons for ....Truly a remarkable book and thank heavens you recorded it...."
   ~Andy Enefer, distant relative of Minnie Rose, Verwood, Dorset, UK

"....From nesting, egg laying, hatching, chick care and hen psychology, through basic poultry room and board, Minnie Rose is with you every step of the way...."
~Kathleen Thorne, Adult Program Coord., Kitsap Regional Library, WA

"The perfect book for difficult times....a kind of poetry of the earth and it yields fresh eggs. A wonderfully put-together little book, as it should be."
~Mike Dillon, poet/publisher, Pacific Publishing Co., Seattle, WA

"....charming little book, a veritable bible on how to raise chickens.....It is one of those remarkable strokes of fate that Minnie arranged to sail on the Titanic, but when the ship wasn't ready, came across on another boat...."
~Emmett Watson, *Seattle Post Intelligencer*, April, 1975

"...graphically interesting....illustrations highlight the test..."
Bainbridge Review, May 1975

"....You don't even have to like chickens to find her book....charming and fascinating." **~Ann Combs, author of *Helter Shelter*, April 2009**

"Sometimes the smallest, simplest things can yield the biggest lessons. This is one of those rare books that both inspires and humbles. Lyrical, stripped-down, almost Taoist lessons on life told through such a practical and basic lens. I highly recommend this one!"
~Cedric (Seattle), an *Amazon Review*

"I first met Minnie Rose Lovgreen in the early 1970's....Other than Minnie Rose, who could write about chickens so intimately? Who else could share the mother hen's gentle cooing and clucks whispered to baby chicks inside their shells before hatching?"
~Gerald Elfendahl, Bainbridge Island Historian, Bainbridge Island, WA

"....a tribute to a way of life, and a source of knowledge that so many of us only view with faint curiosity as it fades before our eyes...."
~Ryan Reynolds, *Seward City News*, Feb., 2010

"Minnie Rose knew what she was talking about."
Betsy Leger, book designer and friend of Minnie Rose

Minnie Rose Lovgreen at her dairy farm

Far As
I Can
Remember

An Immigrant Woman's Story, 1888~1975

by

Minnie Rose Lovgreen

Recorded by Nancy Rekow
Edited by Nancy Rekow & Everett Thompson

NW TRILLIUM PRESS
Bainbridge Island, Washington

NW Trillium Press
5591 Battle Point Drive NE
Bainbridge Island, WA 98110
www.nwtrilliumpress.com
editors@nwtrilliumpress.com
(206) 842-6908

ISBN 978-0-9824553-3-3
Library of Congress Control Number: 2010924492
Printed by Color House Graphics, Grand Rapids, Michigan

ILLUSTRATION ACKNOWLEDGMENTS
The following illustrations are used with the kind permission
of the owners indicated below:

Bainbridge Island Historical Society: 88, 121, 137, 149, 151, 155, 158, 172
Nancy Rekow: Cover, IV, 161, 163, 165, 167
Nigel Nudd, Hockwold, Norfolk, Website (www.hockwold.info): 20, 32, 47, 56
64
Website http://oldcarandtruckpictures.com/OldClassicConvertibles: 119
Website www.greatships.net/scans/PC-ME09.jpg: 87

To Elizabeth Hutchison Zwick

gifted illustrator/designer and friend who transformed *Minnie Rose Lovgreen's Recipe for Raising Chickens* into a work of art, and over the years collaborated with Nancy on various books. Now she has helped design this one.

We are most grateful.

Contents

Foreword

An Immigrant Woman's Story

Minnie Rose Lovgreen was a mystery.

How did she–a 19th-century English farm girl and housemaid with next to no education–narrowly miss sinking on the Titanic? How did she learn to read, write, cook, sew, and to nourish children, plants, and animals? How did she escape an abusive husband in the dead of winter? How did she wend her way from England to Canada to Bainbridge Island, Washington? Once there, how did she and her second husband manage to establish and run, for 30 years, a prizewinning dairy that grew to 75 cows on 170 acres?

How did she–dying of cancer at age 86–become the author of a popular book called *Minnie Rose Lovgreen's Recipe for Raising Chickens*? And finally, how did she happen to leave us this dramatic story of her life, *Far As I Can Remember*? How did she achieve all this so many years before Women's Lib? Well," says Minnie Rose–a lifelong storyteller–"I had to use my head for something."

This book tells the story, tape-recorded in her own words three months before she died. Born Minnie Rose Enefer in 1888, "down the fen" in Norfolk County England, she was the eighth of nineteen children on her father's 200-acre wheat farm. When Minnie was four, her mother died and her father soon remarried. From then on, besides hard work on the farm, Minnie's job was to help with the younger children, to "keep the babies from getting under Stepmother's feet."

Minnie Rose Lovgreen

At age eleven, Minnie took matters into her own hands and left home, setting out on the first of her many adventures. As she says, "I was all looking ahead."

Meeting Minnie Rose Lovgreen, decades later and on another continent, changed my life. But I could not have foreseen that. I'd grown up loving nature and books on an old fruit farm in New Jersey. With a BA in English from Oberlin College, I worked for Harcourt, Brace Publishers in New York, earned an MA in Education and taught grade school, then lived two years in England teaching for USAF, where I met and married Ken Rekow, an intelligence officer from Minnesota.

In 1964, Ken and I, both nature-lovers, bought an old dairy farm on Bainbridge Island, WA, from Charlie and Celine Clayton, who'd run a dairy there over 35 years. The farm, with apple and filbert trees, had a southwest pasture that sloped down to a creek surrounded by bigleaf maples and firs. There were weathered outbuildings–a big old hay barn, a milking barn and a milk shed. We never operated a dairy, though we did have beef cattle. And there was a big old chicken coop. So naturally we got some chickens.

Ken,an attorney, commuted by ferry to Seattle every weekday. But he also did most of the farm work, having spent much time on his grandparents' farms in Minnesota.

Soon after we moved in, an elderly woman with an English accent started phoning. She said her name was Minnie Rose Lovgreen. She said she was an old friend of Celine Clayton's. She said she lived up the road. She said she had a German shepherd named Prince we might like for a watchdog. Would we want to come see him?

At first, mired down with moving and settling in, we didn't pay much attention. But Minnie Rose kept phoning. And phoning. An English accent. And phoning. And did we have chickens? Yes, we did. Then maybe we'd like to come see her chickens. Well, maybe. Finally one weekend we drove up the road to visit, with our three-year-old daughter, Sara.

Minnie Rose was then 74. She bustled around and showed us her chickens, her chicken coop, her sheep, her apple trees, her vegetable garden, and Prince, her German shepherd. She picked us peapods fresh off the vines. She talked and she talked every step of the way. Meanwhile her husband, Leo, stood quietly under an apple tree, talking with Ken and smoking his pipe.

I was young. Little did I know. Here was this old woman in flowered housedress and apron who talked non-stop in her unique English accent, who dyed her hair red, who never seemed to stop talking. I was pregnant. I was tired. But obviously she did know some things. Finally we drove off with Prince, who did turn out to be a good watchdog.

That August our son Alec was born. That winter it rained. The sky was gray. The kids kept catching colds. I was lonely. And Minnie Rose kept calling. What to do, I asked her, for the fevers, the sore throats, the earaches? What to do with the firstborn chicks that always seemed to hatch out when my husband was away on a business trip? She offered her often creative solutions. And they always seemed to work. Soon I began to phone Minnie Rose with farm and garden questions too. And I found out others were phoning her with questions. She always loved sharing her wisdom.

One spring day, holding our third baby, Mitch, I watched Minnie Rose gently insert two fluffy, peeping young chicks into Sara's and Alec's coat sleeves. "There," she said. "Feel how soft and warm. It's cozy in there, just like under the mother hen."

Right then I said, "Minnie Rose, do you ever babysit?"

"Oh, my dear," she said. "I've been taking care of children all my life."

Minnie Rose Lovgreen

So Minnie Rose, by then a widow, became our babysitter and friend. And she certainly had her ways with children. Fixing a bowl of oatmeal, she'd scoop holes, fill them with milk, and call it a duck pond. For a snack, she'd spread a slice of bread with peanut butter, and serve it cut into strips she called "ladyfingers." In late August, she'd have our kids bring slabs of cardboard to toboggan wildly down the steep hill of brown, sundried grass behind her house.

She sang old songs and chanted old rhymes. She told stories of folk and fairies, frogs and cream. But best of all, she told stories of her own incredible life, begun as a motherless, hardworking farm girl in England, then sailing over an ocean to a new life. She told her stories matter-of-factly, cheerfully, but we learned how hard she'd worked and how, when her life got hard, she'd always invented solutions.

In January, 1975, Minnie Rose was diagnosed with cancer and hospitalized in Seattle for tests. I rode the ferry into Seattle, appeared in her hospital room with a tape-recorder, and said, "Okay, Minnie Rose, now we're going to start your book." She'd always wanted to write a book on how to raise chickens, but was always much too busy.

So Minnie Rose lay in that white bed, in that white room, and dictated all her chicken-keeping secrets. In the weeks that followed I transcribed, then decided to hand-letter, her words.

One day our friend Elizabeth Hutchison Zwick—chicken-raiser on a nearby farm–said she'd like to illustrate Minnie Rose's book. I'd had no idea this very capable farmwoman was also an artist! She showed me her beautiful drawings of plants, animals and children. "Yes. Please be the illustrator," I said.

Elizabeth illustrated Minnie Rose's words with original pen and ink drawings of Minnie's farm–of chickens, coops, setting hens, chicks, and fighting roosters. With those exquisite drawings, and her creative ideas about format, Elizabeth transformed the book from text only into a work of art.

We had no time to spare that spring. Because we knew Minnie Rose was dying, we worked long, long hours. One afternoon I took Minnie Rose out for a drive along Puget Sound. She sat in back with my four-year-old daughter, Rebecca, who knew she was very ill. After a quiet stretch, Rebecca said to Minnie, "You're going to die some time."

Minnie Rose didn't skip a beat. She said, "Yes, dear. Just like the flowers."

That April of 1975 I published the book. Both the title (*Recipe for Raising Chickens*) and the subtitle (*The Main Thing Is To Keep Them Happy*) were Minnie own words.

Minnie Rose died that July. But not before she appeared on King TV, not before she signed books at an autograph party, and not before she knew her book was selling widely to chicken-raisers and book lovers across the country.

Our 1,000 copies sold out in a month! What to do? With four young children, I had little time to market the book (not to mention know-how). I showed the book to Pacific Search Press in Seattle, who took it on and printed 20,000 copies. After Minnie's death, her book continued to sell until 1988, then was out of print over 20 year—until May, 2009, when Everett Thompson and I published a 3rd edition.

As of now, May, 2010, *Minnie Rose Lovgreen's Recipe for Raising Chickens* has sole over 24,000 copies. Would Minnie Rose have been surprised? Perhaps not, because she knew her chicken-raising advice really worked. But she certainly would have been pleased and proud.

Now about this book you hold in your hands. Back in 1975, after tape-recording Minnie's chicken wisdom, she and I went on to record her whole life story. I transcribed it all, but then it sat in my files for 35 years. At last now, as I promised her, we

Minnie Rose Lovgreen

are pleased to publish Minnie's second book, *Far As I Can Remember: An Immigrant Woman's Story, 1888-1975.*

As co-editors, Everett and I have preserved Minnie's original words as she spoke them in her unique storytelling voice, which simmers and jumps and sings along. Here and there, for clarity, we've changed or added a word or punctuation. And sometimes, because she often backtracked or leaped ahead, we've moved sections around to maintain continuity. Hers was a conversational style all her own— spirited, dramatic, humorous, opinionated and wise.

Minnie Rose loved telling her life story. We hope you enjoy reading it.

Nancy Rekow, June, 2010

Chapter One

1888-1899

England~Wheat Farm~Nineteen Children~Stepmother

~ *"My own mother died when I was four."*
~ *"You didn't waste nothing on the farm."*
~ *"Sparrows and blackbirds could go in pies. And larks."*

My father farmed over two hundred acres. But it wasn't his land, you know. He'd rented it from his father. And then, after, his father died, and left so much for each son. But he couldn't no more work that land after we was all gone—because you take my six brothers, you know, digging in there every day, working away to get things fixed up....

A wheat farm is seasonal. You have to plow your land early in the spring. Then you have to watch out for the seasons. When the wheat is ripe you have to be ready to get it down, and you always hope the weather will stay right. We were wheat farmers. That was what we did. That was our main thing, was wheat. We sold wheat all over England.

My father had white hair and a little mustache. And he never grew a beard. He was medium sized. And then my stepmother was a big robust woman. She stood about pretty near six feet, really broad and husky, you know. She was a strong girl, that's one thing. Almost like the Scandinavians. As a matter of fact, her name was Richardson before she was married, so she was probably from a Scandinavian family.

My own mother's name was Mary Ann Harrison, so she was from Scandinavian people too, or something, anyway. She died when I was four. They was a musical family on that side, on her side. They all seemed to be quite musical on her side. But on my stepmother's side they was not musical. They couldn't understand how you could hit a note and make it sound like anything.

My brothers all played. One played the accordion and one played the violin. They played at weddings and played at different things around for entertainment. Zach, he played at weddings and that. He played the violin. And then Sidney had the accordion. We used to have great times with Sid, because he'd get that accordion going, you know, and he'd play that accordion. And then some of them played the harmonica. Jess sang more than he played. He had a very clear voice, he could start right up.

I played the piano and I also sang. But we didn't have a piano in our home, so I picked it up as I went along. Wherever I worked they let me play on the piano, see, and I picked up music by ear. I still play by ear. I took notes for a while, so I could help the children with theirs, but it seemed like I didn't go too far with that, I didn't gain too much. But singing was one of my things, because if I couldn't remember a piece of

16

poetry, I'd put a tune to it, and then I could remember it. So then I got so I'd translate it into a story, you know, because that was all because I wasn't going to school. I had to use my head for something.

I don't think I went to school six months in all my life. I don't think I did. I didn't know I could count back until we had the dairy business. I didn't know I could count change back. I got counting money and then it came to me, and someone said, "Well, where did you get your education from? You've been in business before." They saw me counting back and I thought, oh goodness, thank goodness they didn't discover I never had any schooling.

My oldest brother's name was Zachariah. And the next one was Herbert John. Zachariah was one who liked to work on the farm. Herbert John was in the militia. He went with the war service, like the reservists, where they had the little pillbox hats, you know, that strapped under their chin, and blue pants with a yellow or an orange stripe down.

Then Frederick Russell, he was one of the head horsemen. We had nine big workhorses, so he had to help take care of the horses. And then there was Sidney Charles. He was the second horseman. So if one horseman happened to be away, the other one had to do the whole thing. So they had to be efficient. Horses had to be handled very carefully. They weren't banging them around or anything like that. They just treated them as if they were human beings, and then more of a coaxing habit with them. They coaxed them along and humored them.

And if a horse was going to have a baby, why my brother set up all night with the horse to make sure that she didn't need any help. And he slept in this wagon of straw out there. Even in the wintertime, they'd sleep in the wagon of straw and cover up, you know. So if the horse was going to have her colt, why they could get up and help her. It always happened in the nighttime. They don't seem to have their babies during the day.

My brother Jess worked for other people as well as working at home. He worked at home a little bit, but he worked for other people. They didn't seem to have a job for him at home. He had worked for some people and he met a girl, and he was very fond of this girl. He knew it wouldn't be any use to stay around home, because he wouldn't make enough money to support a wife or anything, so he went to Canada real early. Sold his pigs and went to Canada.

And then after he'd been in Canada for a while, he came home and married a girl he went to school with. And so he married her, and then they lived in England for a while, and after a while they had a baby and the baby died. I didn't know what the baby died of—got a cold or something like that.

And so after that, well, he decided he'd go back to Canada again. So he went back to Canada, and he stayed in Canada all the time. He found work there, working on those machines that fixed the roads and stuff like that, you know. Whatever work there was, he was always happy to be on it. He was a strong man.

Irene (my niece) came along after that. And Jess's wife died when Irene was nine years old. Then Irene was raised by another lady there, a neighbor that said she would take care of Irene if she'd go and live at her house. So Irene stayed there, and Jess, her father, boarded there, too, so they both boarded there. And that way it worked out very well because, after Irene's mother died, Irene got educated there, went to school there and got her music and everything. And then later on when she got grown up, she came to stay with me for three months when we was over here in the U.S.

And then Alfred Escott. He was coming along where he could feed calves and help to clean the stalls out and everything like that. My father thought he was the most wonderful little boy out, because he was always willing to do things. So we had a little cow that had a small, small calf. Father said that calf wasn't much good, it was too small to even think about raising it.

So my brother Alfred would hurry up and eat his breakfast and get out there and see if he couldn't encourage that little calf to eat some more, so it would grow up. And my father noticed how interested he was in the little calf, so finally he said, "I'll give you that calf." He said, "You being so good about trying to look after it and doing the other work, why I'll give you that calf, and it can stay here and grow up, and when it gets all full grown you can sell it."

Well, it grew up and it had a pair of twins, and so it was really something. It was a little white calf with a black nose. Holstein and Guernsey, I think, or White Swiss or something like that, but anyways it was a small breed calf. So when Alfred sold all them, the mother and the twins, then he had enough money to go to Canada with.

He and I, we always worked together. We were just like twins at home. There was about one year's difference between

19

us, but he was always very good about looking after us and trying to do things for us.

We couldn't have any apples. There was a big apple orchard, and him and I both got to go to work in the apple orchard. But we weren't to take any apples home. You couldn't take any home unless you bought some. So he bought a half a bushel of apples, carried them home on his back in a sack, put them upstairs in a locker, in a little box, and locked it up. He had a little box there that he put them in and locked up.

He'd give everybody an apple every night so they could have an apple. That was his idea. That was something no one else couldn't have any control over. That was his apples. He bought them and paid for them. He always believed that what you worked for that was what you had. So the apples didn't have a chance to go bad. He gave us one every night.

**Hockwold, Norfolk, a village near the Enefer
family's farm on the River Little Ouse**

That's the brother I went to Canada with after a while. He went early first and worked in Canada for a while, and then he came back and married the girl that he went to school with. He went to school a little bit, so he married the girl he went to school with. But he wanted to go back. He said he didn't like England after he'd been in Canada. So he asked me (later) if I'd like to go along, because his wife wouldn't go unless I would go. So I decided (later) I'd go, right in a hurry. It was so nice because we'd always worked together.

The younger brothers would be from the second family. And they were just growing up when I left, about five or six years old. One was named Bert and the other one was Walter. And Elijah and George. I think that's all. Let's see. Yes, they're the boys. And then there was two girls, Mary and Ellen.

You see, I was the eighth of nineteen children. I had to try and help take care of all of them, so that was one thing I wanted to leave home for, because there was too many. I couldn't handle them all. Some of them wanted to do things, and some of them liked to and some of them didn't like to. And when they didn't like me, well then, I didn't want to be home.

My older sisters, one of them went as a mother's helper for a while. Her name was Edith May. She worked for the same couple I did later, the Sheltons, in Ely. Edith May was the oldest girl at home, so she was like a mother to us younger children, and she wanted us to call her "Mother," but we didn't want to call her "Mother." So she didn't like it very much, and she was pretty near always angry at us for some reason or other because we wouldn't call her "Mother." So she left the place and went to work.

21

And then Georgiana was the next one. Georgiana went to the same place, the Sheltons'. She was helper there at the same place. Well, she got so she got a little bit too big for her job, she thought. So she got another job. And then I went there. I went there later on. And I stayed longer than any of them did, because I liked the job, and I was younger, of course, to go and start out. And they liked me, and we got along real good.

Our house was made of brick, with a thatched roof. It had to be a good-sized house, for so many in the family, but it wasn't fancy, just strong and solid. Those houses didn't have too many fissures, because they all stood on the ground. They was warm built because most of them was brick. The windows weren't very big because they let too much cold in. There were about two windows in the living room. And then in the kitchen they had two big windows there.

The furniture was bought. It was pretty good old-style furniture. All carved and everything. No one hardly ever ate in the kitchen. We always ate in the living room. Our floor in the living room was big square tiles. They were red, like red bricks. And they sprinkled sand on the floor, so that if the floor got dirty when you walked around, the dirt would mix in with the sand. Then you'd sweep up the sand and you'd swept the dirt up too. Then we'd put clean sand down. I don't know where we got the sand from, but there didn't seem to be any problem about the sand.

We had a big round table, a huge round table, and chairs. And if the chairs didn't fit up against the round table, then those that had a vacant place would have to stand and eat. So my brother and I usually stood in corners to eat our meal when the whole family was there, and then we could go out and play after. But they always sang grace before meals and sang grace after meals, too.

My father had an armchair, like they do you know, the old armchairs, with a cushion in, and some of them had a little cushion they put down the back and some of them didn't. And Stepmother didn't have a big armchair like that. She had another chair there and my father set both up at the same end of the table. He pulled up in his chair and then after he had his dinner or his breakfast or whatever it was, then he always leaned back in his chair and had a little smoke with his pipe. And then he went out.

Meals was boiled suet puddings and boiled pork, salt pork, and potatoes and carrots—that was our big meal. We had that in the middle of the day, because everyone was home on the farm, so. And then at nighttime we had celery and butter and lettuce or radishes, and that was the evening meal. It was always bread and butter and raw vegetables. That would be about five thirty in the evening. For breakfast, I think the men mostly had bacon or cold salty pork and maybe cold boiled potatoes, bread and butter and milk.

And then when we got up, we had a bowl of bread and milk each. And most of us had tea, one cup or mug of tea each, with sugar in it. And sometimes the water wasn't quite boiling so the tea wasn't too appetizing, but anyway we drank it. We didn't usually drink milk exceptin' we had it in pudding or for bread and milk. Bread and milk was when you'd soak two pieces of bread in a bowl and cover it with warm milk, put brown sugar on that, and made your breakfast. We liked that.

Minnie Rose Lovgreen

No one got much fruit those days. My stepmother didn't know how to can any fruit, and we didn't know how to can any fruit, so we had to eat whatever fruit was in season. She made jam sometimes. No one had any fruit. There was an orange at Christmastime, and of course you could have carrots and raw turnips and stuff like that. That was our vegetable. That was really what we used in place of fruit. And we had nuts at Christmas, and we didn't have them any other time.

On Sunday, we usually had a baked Yorkshire pudding and sometimes roast beef, but we hardly ever got beef on Sundays unless we got some stewed meat and boiled that. Beef was so expensive that we couldn't afford to have it, so we ate pork from one year's end to the other. Every day, every day, pork. We raised our own pigs and salted them down, and took the salt pork and rinsed it off, and put it in to boil over a fire. We used turf—that was peat moss. We just had to keep that salt pork simmering. We made it boil real good, and then we kept the fire under to keep it simmering.

There was a little stove in the living room where Stepmother would put some coal on the fire sometimes and then back that up a little bit. Then you could get the oven hot a little bit, enough to make a Yorkshire pudding in or maybe some buns. We called them buns, but they were like little cakes, with raisins in or currants. That was only a little fancy fireplace stove, one that you'd put blacking on and shine it. It didn't hardly have any top on it. Well, it did have a little lid so you could stand a teakettle on it. And we made a rug and put it in front of the fire. It was a pegged rug, made from strips of wool cloth.

So, if they wanted to lay the baby on the rug in front of the fire, you had to put some kind of a screen so there wasn't any sparks to fly out, because if you had a little fire it was either turf or coal. My stepmother would lay the baby in front of the fire.

I remember one woman, I'll never forget it. She laid her baby on the rug in front of the fire and she went out bike riding. She knew the baby couldn't crawl any further and she never thought. And somehow or other, I don't know what she had on the fire, but somehow or other something blew out of the fire and blew on the baby and the baby got burned to death. And oh, how people did storm about that woman. They said she was gadding around there on her bike instead of looking after her baby, and so on and so forth.

But the other stove where we cooked the puddings and things was over an open fireplace. We built the turf in the fireplace, and got it boiling that way. And we had bellows to blow the turfs to make them burn till they got good flame. And the Dutch oven–it was a huge Dutch oven that could hold the whole meal–held the pork and the potatoes, and carrots and everything. It was a great big heavy kettle with a handle over the top so you could hang it up the chimney on a chain. When it boiled it usually kept boiling, because you banked the fire up just enough to keep the turf burning. Turf would keep going a long time. Peat moss smolders, you know, and just keeps going for a long time.

We had a man specially dig out the peat moss, just like a long row of bricks. He dug them out every spring, and then they stayed there all summer getting dry. Then in the fall we took them into a shed, and we called that the turf shed. You might call it the woodshed here, but we called it the turf shed there. And we stacked them all up in there, and that supply had to last us all winter. So people didn't set up and burn fires. They just went to bed when they wanted to.

We had kerosene lamps, and candles, and we had to clean the glasses most every day. If we carried the lamps and let the glasses get smoked up, then we had to clean them, so we got to be pretty careful about how we carried the lamps around. And there were lanterns, of course, to go outside to do the animals with.

Of course, they sold all their furniture much later when they came to Canada. They had a cupboard there that I thought a lot of. It was almost like one of them pendulum clocks with all the ornaments on it, and I'd left it there, and two little mirrors, because someone had given it to me, and I thought my brother would take care of it, but they sold all the stuff. I didn't hear no more about it. I didn't want the money for it so much as I liked it.

There was a huge fireplace in the kitchen. It was all brick. And the brick oven was alongside of it. The brick oven had to be beautifully made so it didn't smoke or anything like that. There was a big table too, like a kitchen queen, that had drawers in it, and a place to knead the bread on. It was always kept scrupulously clean. It was scrubbed down.

And the floors were scrubbed. They didn't have any linoleum on the floors. And no linoleum on the table covers, either. The kitchen floor was bricks or tiles, and they'd be sinking in, and we'd have to adjust them every once in a while.

They were getting pretty old. And they were nice to walk on. They always looked nice, cozy and everything, on the tile floor in front of the fireplace.

Upstairs we had beds where two or three girls got into one bed, and maybe two or three in another bed, and if there wasn't enough blankets they put gunnysacks over, brand new gunnysacks. My father used to buy a whole lot of new gunnysacks when he sacked the wheat up, so before he used the sacks why we could have them upstairs and put them on our beds.

When the boys went up to their room, all they had up there was beds. They didn't have very many clothes, so they didn't need any clothes closets. When they took their clothes off, they'd put them under the mattress to have them real straight, so they were all pressed for Sunday, so their creases all stayed in them, see. But no one had any fancy clothes.

And there was wooden floors upstairs. You could hear them screeching. The girls went up a little winding staircase, but where the boys went up it was just like a ladder. They climbed up a ladder and went through a hole just like you'd be going up to an attic. Stepmother couldn't get up there very easily, so she didn't try to go up. She used to send me up to make the beds, and if I'd be a long time making the beds, she'd be wondering what I was doing.

The babies had a cradle. And then we had a big iron crib that was quite big, so you could put three in one end and two in the other. So there was some heads up one end and more heads up the other. And the feet touched each other. They put their feet against each other and kept each others' feet warm. The cribs would rock, so if you had to get the children to sleep, you'd stand and rock and that would make them go to sleep.

And of course they had outside toilets. Even when they came to Canada (years later), my father didn't believe in having the toilet in the house or anywhere near the house. He thought that was most unsanitary. I remember a funny story when my brother got married. He was always so particular about his food. If a fly happened to settle on anything he was going to eat, or a frog went past right then, he wouldn't want to eat that any more no matter what.

So one day—him and his wife moved you know after they got married—they was on a little farm of their own—and one day the bread man came. He only came once a week. Well, when he brought the bread wagon around, he couldn't find nobody home. Both the doors was locked. So he put the bread in the toilet outside. And when my brother come home, he knew that they were out of bread and he knew that Harry Flat should have come along and brought the bread. Then they went to the toilet and saw the bread there. So my brother said Harry could just fetch all of it back, because he wouldn't have anything of it. So they had to fetch all of it back.

We all got along pretty well with each other, my brothers and I. And then, of course, when they had to go do the afternoon chores, everybody helped feed the calves and everything. And I had to go in and help with the children. I had to keep the babies from getting under Stepmother's feet. She always wanted to not have her babies crawling around where she was working. She couldn't seem to stand that. She had us, though. She was lucky to have us to do those things for her.

I had to learn to keep babies entertained. I'd make them little things, little objects. Or I'd take rushes, and take the pulp out, and make everlasting flowers and stuff like that. They liked something to bring in the house, something that would decorate the house.

And I told them stories. There was one about the frogs and the cream. There was two little frogs and they saw a crock of cream (half a crock) standing there, and they both was hungry for the cream. They climbed up the side of the crock, the jar, and one put his foot in to taste the cream. And then he fell in and he couldn't get out because it was slippery. The other one thought he'd go and help him out, and then he fell in, too. Then they were both in. They kicked and kicked and struggled to try to climb up to get out, but their hands were so full of the cream that they slipped back in every time.

Then finally one little frog said, "Well, I think I'll give up. I'll give up. I can't make it." Then the other one said, "I aim to keep kicking away, and if I die I'll die kicking." So he kicked away until the cream turned into butter. Then they both stood on the butter and climbed out.

And we played "hide the stick" up in the haystack, or hiding something else and looking all around and getting warmer and warmer, almost like an Easter egg hunt. And we made our own dolls out of alder. We had to make our own dolls and dress them with things out in the woods. Well, you just took a little branch, and this little branch had two little arms sticking out, and then you took leaves for a dress. You picked out the leaf, then folded the leaf over, and then pinched a little piece out of the top and slipped that over the head like a little chemise. And then you put another leaf around for the skirt, and you held that together with a piece of grass or a piece of hay. So those were our dolls.

And we made whistles, you know, out of alder. They made their own whistles, the boys did. And they had tennis or something like that they played. Some kind of ball game. But we always had to stay in our own yard. We couldn't ever go in other people's places. Father said it was better for us to stay in our own yard.

I noticed Stepmother always put a lot of lilac in the house when it was lilac time. She would put a lot of lilac all around. The house would smell real nice. And we had marigolds and a few roses. And a plant called "old man." It's kind of a brush, like sage. You'd smell it, and it smelled different than anything else. It was a sage color, but they called it "old man" because it was kind of gray. And it smelled awful pretty and was a little bush.

One time when my sister came home, she said she was sure that I could fly, that I was light enough to fly, specially when I had one of them little dresses on that was flounced out at the bottom. So she put me up on a big haystack, and she pinned a brown paper on each of my shoulders. And she said, "Now, when that next gust of wind comes you be all ready to zoom." Well the gust of wind came and I wasn't all ready to zoom, so I didn't go that time. "Now," she says, "you didn't do it. Now, watch for the next time."

I must have been about six and she was about nine or ten. Her name was Edith May. So her and Georgiana—that was the other sister—they were both there on the stack, you know. "Soon as the next gust of wind come," she said, "now, be all ready to go." And she gave me a push. So then I fell slap down between two trees. And I remember the expression on her face. She said, "Oh, she didn't fly, she didn't fly!"

I never saw my sisters after they grew up, until I went back home to England in 1955.

One job I always had to do was wash off all the diapers. the way they did on the babies' diapers was the one that was next to the baby got washed, but the one that was next to that one, that got dried and used over again. So you didn't really run out. You couldn't let yourself run out of diapers.

We had an old barrel outside they kept half full of water. And as soon as a diaper was taken off the baby—they didn't know anything about diaper brushes or scrubbin' 'em off first or anything like that—it was put in there. Babies' diapers—and there was always a baby—went in that barrel.

And then it was my job after breakfast to go out there and start fishing out the diapers, and then washing off all the soil, and then washing all them diapers, and then bringing them in for Stepmother to finish them off. But she didn't want them in all soiled, so I had to stay out there and wash them, and the water was pretty cold in winter. When it was icy they froze over, you know. But I still had to, and my hands were bleeding on the back. But it didn't matter how cold the water was. That was my job. Those were the things that didn't make any difference. You grew up with them. You knew it was your job. I was discouraged over it. It didn't matter what you'd do.

Minnie Rose Lovgreen

**Minnie Rose hauled water from the River Little Ouse
to wash babies' diapers for her stepmother.**

Whenever there was a quarrel, it was always sending me upstairs to look after a baby that would scream and say, "Come back I'm not asleep yet." Those were the things that got me, and then I could hear them quarreling downstairs.   And that's why I finally run away. I couldn't stand the argument and quarreling. I couldn't stand people quarreling. If I can't help them when they're quarreling, I get out of there. I was always that way.I was sensitive to that. And they knew me me for that.

One time when my hands got real bad and bleeding from doing those diapers, my father said he was going to get us some Vaseline. But Stepmother wouldn't hear of letting us use the Vaseline. She said it was wastin' money. So he got some Vaseline and hid it up in the cow barn and told us where it was, so we could go and rub some on our hands whenever she didn't know anything about it. He hid it up in the cow barn 'cause he used to use some for the cows, and for his own hands, too. He was a kind man, but he wanted to keep peace among the family, you see, so that was the way he always was. I had to get water out of the river to wash clothes with, and we had a pair of yokes on our shoulders, and they had a chain on each side, and you'd carry two buckets of water, and you'd balance for carrying them up over the bank. So I had to go and fill those pails at the river, and bring up two pails of water (at a time), and maybe about twenty to thirty pails of water for them to put in a big barrel for Stepmother to use for washday, before I could do anything else.

Churning the butter was another regular job. I had to churn the butter. Stepmother said it was my job to churn. I used to get up in the summertime and start churning for butter real early before the sun got up. If Father got up before Stepmother did, then he'd come and give a few turns. It took probably a half hour or a little bit more. It'd depend on the cream. Sometimes it'd take over an hour. Sometimes I'd churn for an hour and the butter wouldn't come.

The churn was a great big barrel churn. The top would churn. It stood on a frame like a sawhorse almost, a frame that was made on purpose for it. We turned a handle and it kept going over and over and over. And it had a cork in it. Every once in a while you'd have to take the cork out and let the air out and then put the cork back in again. The cork had a piece of rag around it, so it would easy come out and it didn't let the cream out. And then we'd turn it.

Minnie Rose Lovgreen

And if you started in, if it was cool enough and you started in pretty fast with it, well you'd get it started good. But then you'd have to start slowing up when you thought it was coming, so that the butter came all in little crumbles, and then you'd keep on and on till it collected up, you know, made into it.

When the butter had come, then you could let the buttermilk out. You'd let the buttermilk out of where you opened that cork. But you couldn't let it out until it collected up some. The buttermilk all had to go in to the pigs.

People never thought about drinking buttermilk them days. Nobody even heard of such a thing. You didn't waste nothing on the farm. Everything went to something. After you let out the buttermilk, then you could put some water in the churn and you could even wash the butter in the churn by churning it some more, but you had to churn it easy, not just flip it around, you know.

Then there was a bigger hole—I didn't used to have to get in that—there was a bigger hole that they took off some kind of a little spring there that was clamped, and they took the butter out there. They took it out by the handfuls, you know. It was nice and solid. And then they put it in a big wooden bowl with a little salt and water, and they'd wash it and wash it until all the milk was out of it. Then they'd have to squash it around till there was no water left in.

Then Stepmother made it up into pounds, clapped it together, and clapped the ends together. Then she had a little wooden thing, a butter print, with a wheel on. She'd run that across the top and that made roses on it, rose design, same as the butter.

If it was wintertime when the cows wasn't getting any grass, the butter was very pale. So she took carrots and we scraped the carrots and she squeezed them through a cheesecloth and put that carrot juice in the butter. And that made it the color that it ought to be. See, we had to trade in the butter for groceries—we didn't have any money to buy groceries. Each grocer ordered so much butter for so many groceries according to value.

So we had real good butter that way, and about twice a week we churned. We had to eat butter. And if we had butter on our bread, we didn't have nothing else on it. If we had jam on our bread, we didn't have butter. If we had lard on our bread, we could have a little salt with that. And if they had cheese on their bread, they didn't have butter either.

I think we only had about thirteen or fourteen cows, you see, but we just kept them for making the butter and stuff like that. We only raised a beef one once in a while. In fact if we raised a beef one, it had to be sold to pay other expenses, because we couldn't afford to eat the beef, we had to eat pork. There wasn't any inspection and the cows didn't have to be tied in anywhere to go to milk. They were gentle and they knew us, and so we'd just go with a stool and set down by them anywhere and they'd stay there till they were milked, chewing their cuds, you know.

Then in summertime when they went out to grass, of course the butter was a beautiful color when they got on the grass. Almost a buttercup. Almost a buttercup yellow.

Minnie Rose Lovgreen

Each day at milking time when they scummed the cream off of the milk, they had a thing like you turn the eggs over with, you know, all full of little holes. And the cream was so thick that when they scummed it off the top of those big milk cans, they'd put that in a crock. And they had dug a hole in the ground and stood this crock in the ground, way down fairly deep. They had a big lid they put over it and nothing bothered that. That was to keep the cream until next churning day again, when it was butter day again.

Now we had nine big work horses. They had to be fed about five thirty or six in the morning if they were going to go out at seven thirty to work. We had to make them each a ration, so we had a big round pan–not a pail, but a big round sifter–and we put so much oats in and so much chaff, that was straw chaff, you know, and so much brown mangles, and sometimes beans. We made up a complete ration for each horse and put it in front of them in their manger. And they had to have all that time to eat it and digest it before they went out to work.

For the horses we had rail fences. They were very cautious over the horses, a lot more than over the cows. They were Clydesdales, with the big feet. Some brown and some dapple gray. Most of them was brown. One was called Beauty and one was called Bess. They all went by names–you always knew what you were talking about. They had a stable, and all their harness hung up in their stable, see. Nothin' went in their stable but them. We wouldn't even have a chicken bone in there around where they had to eat.

'Course the horses had to have shoes on. And they had to have their feet trimmed. And then if it was breeding season, they had to watch out that they had the stallion comin' around when the breeding season was, so they would have the foals at the right time. If a horse was lame, or a little bit lame in the shoulder or anything like that, my father wouldn't let it work. And if anyone wanted to borrow a horse from us, he never would rent the horse without renting one of his men with it. He said the horse couldn't talk and he didn't want his horse abused, and he didn't know how they'd use them. So he, he was a good organizer. He was a September man and he was an awful good organizer.

When a mare was expecting a foal, they had to work her some, but not as much. And then if they come in off the field when they were hot, they didn't give them all the water they wanted to drink. They just give them a little and then kept them in, and if they were sweaty they rubbed them down. And they had to be brushed and curried to keep their skin good and clean so that fleas wouldn't breed or anything, you know, or ticks. If a horse was sick and couldn't eat, then you really had to get the veterinary if you couldn't figure out what to do about it.

Well then, light horses, to take people in the buggies when they went to shop and do business, well that was another set of horses. They were treated differently.

If a mare wasn't interested in the horse, and didn't want to conceive, well, they'd take an onion which was called a shallot—that was a very strong little onion—and they'd cut the end off of that. And there was a certain amount of milk or juice

37

come out of that, and they'd rub that around the uterus till they got her so she wanted to have the male. And then she couldn't resist.

And some horses would bite at each other through the fence, you know, to get each other's food. Well then, at lunchtime when they went on the field with them—the men didn't always come in to lunch—they took lunch out to them on the field sometimes–so they took a canvas bag with the horse's lunch, too. And then the horse could eat when the people were eating, and that was a lighter ration than they had in the morning and in the evening. They were all kept in wonderful shape.

Then my father, he went somewhere, and he was quite a horse fancier. So he bought himself a very beautiful riding horse. He didn't ride a great deal, but he just loved to see a beautiful riding horse with beautiful features. Well, he bought that one, and then there was another one that was almost like that, but it wasn't, it didn't have that same character, the same standing or anything. But it had always been a pair with the other horse. So he bought 'em both and he brought 'em home, and he said to my brother: "Now," he said, "you've always been so faithful with the horses. Now," he said, "Violet is mine and Fanny will be yours." He was goin' to give that other to my brother. That was kind of a sad story in the end.

And so my brother was so grateful that his father thought enough of him to give him a horse. He never had gone to school, and he was about eighteen or nineteen years old then. So he said, "What shall I do with the horses now?"

And Father said, "Turn 'em out on the pasture rights, and they'll be happy out there, you know, both together.

So they turned them out on the pasture rights, and the next day his very beautiful horse that he'd paid so much for got sunk in a hole with its right leg and broke its leg and had to be shot. There wasn't a thing to do about it. And my brother said he felt so bad about it, you know, but it was Father's decision— he said turn 'em out on the pasture, and he never thought about 'em gettin' in any of them holes. The ground was soft because it was between the river and the bank. There was lots and lots of grass and it looked beautiful, but if the horses weren't used to that, why then they'd go along and step in this hole.

So then my brother said, "Well, Father, you have my horse now then."

Father said, "No, I won't," he said. "A gift is a gift." And something he'd done to take that punishment. He always believed that if somepin' went wrong, then God was punishing him for somepin' he'd done, and he always had to spend all kinds of time figuring about what he'd done wrong that God punished him for. But he wouldn't take my brother's horse. So that was that.

We had a huge pond of water, and my youngest brother was leading a horse out to give it some water from the pond, and it saw its picture in the water and it went off on a stampede. And he had a rope tied to the horse's neck and a snooze knot around his wrist, and the horse pulled and he got thrown down and pulled and pulled, They went through the nettles and through the brambles, and I stood and screamed

39

and screamed for help till someone came out, and then by that time the horse had gotten through the nettles and through the blackberry thorns, and then the horse stopped. And they went and picked my brother up and I thought sure that he was dead, but he was still alive.

That was one thing I always told our children—if they ever have a horse, never to have a snooze rope around their wrist—have it in your hand, so if the horse does get away, let go. That was Alfred, my younger brother, the one that grew up with me like steps, you know. He was a year younger than I was.

And the first of May, we had water rights or wash rights. Each side of the bank, and our side, on the Norfolk side, was our pasture rights. They were handed down from our ancestors from away back. We couldn't sell them, I don't think. They were pasture rights. So you could turn your cattle out on the first of May. So the farmers got up real early, so the cows could go out and get the first few bites, which sounded kinda' silly, but that's the way they did.

My father milked some, and my brother Jess, he milked some. And whoever. The horsemen didn't milk the cows. They were special horsemen. The one that was Sagittarius was the head horseman. The second horseman was his brother that was next to him in age.

When we butchered the pigs, you had a great big wagon there and you put a barrel of water at the bottom of the wagon. So after they butchered the pig, they took his hind legs and held him over this barrel and socked him up and down and they scraped the fur off. Two or three could be doing it if you had two or three scrapers. It didn't take no time. Then they hung them outside with a blanket around them or something around them to keep the draft off, and so all the blood would absolutely run off, and the carcass was nice and white and pretty. It was really pretty meat by the time you got through with it.

We used the feet for pickled pigs' feet, and the head for head cheese, and of course, all the rest of it. Some of it went into roasts—pork loin went into roasts–and the other bacons and stuff like that. Sometimes they smoked the bacons, and sometimes they didn't. Sometimes they took the bacon and salted it down, you know, and had it for boiling pork. It would be fat, but just the same the surface fat came off, but the other fat didn't. It was still fat pork, see. It wasn't all lean. We didn't get tired of pork, but we didn't like to have to eat the flank. And they used mustard with it, and pickled beets and pickled onions, and stuff like that to help the pork down. But they always depended on the pork.

They were mostly white pigs, the Yorkshire or the Berkshire with the long backs. And Stepmother made sausage out of some of the meat. I don't know which part she used for sausage, but she ground the sausage, ground it up and made sausage. Maybe she ground the liver in with it too. I imagine she did after she washed it real good. Then they took the insides of the pig too, that was all the entrails, and they washed them, and turned them, and washed them, and turned them, and then they'd fill them full of sausage meat. See, that made the casing.

Another chore I did was for the baking. We didn't have any sticks or wood to build a fire with, so we had to manage with what we had, with the dry willows. My brother and I used to have to cut willows with a little ax, each an armful, as much as we could carry. Then as soon as the bread came out of the oven, the big brick oven, we had to fill the oven full of these willows. They were green, and the stored heat left in the oven dried the leaves on the willows so they were like paper then, all parched up. Then next bread day, all you had to do was put a match to them and the leaves served as paper.

We baked bread three times a week. There was nineteen of us finally, so we baked nine loaves at a time. You put a match to the willows, just maybe about fifteen minutes or so ahead of time. When the bread was up by the top of the pan, then it was ready to go in. You put a match to the willows, and when the willows had all burned out, the oven was real hot then. It was just right for the bread, so they put the bread in right away in this brick oven.

The oven was about three foot wide and about five foot long, and so deep that you had to put the first lot of bread in with a shovel because you couldn't reach way back there. They put the loaves three and three and three, and if there was any room to spare, they put a little custard or something in one end of the oven.

Then they raked out some of the extra ashes to keep the heat in. They had a tin door that went in front of where they put the willows in. So they put that up and then they banked those extra ashes up against it to keep the heat in. They knew how long a time before the bread was done because it cooked in stored heat. Then we'd all go out on the land to work, and when we came home the bread was all done. Nothing

42

happened. It didn't burn, you see. It baked beautifully. There was even crusts running over and baked on the side that we used to like to break off and have with butter. I thought that was real good.

When the bread was done, they took it out, and my brother and I had to get the willows all ready again, so that the next bread day they would be all ready to bake, because that was our job. We each had a little ax and we had to go to the ditches, the creeks where the willows was growing, and come up with each a big armful.

I think we was each about seven or eight years old then. Then when the bread came out of the oven, the brick oven, we had to fill it again with all these willows. And we never could fail. They always had to be there, because there wouldn't be anything to bake the bread with when it was done. There was no wood, we had no wood.

And, you know, they had something growing there called faggots. It was a prickly thing almost like a thistle. It grew up like a Scotch broom, but more straight. And when they cut that down, they put bands around that—wire bands or something—and they stood them all up in a row like pillows, and that made the outside of sheds for calves or pigs. They didn't try to eat them because they had prickles on them. But that was quite warm you see, because they was thick like a pillow, they was quite thick.

And then they put a rail so that would hold them up. So that was how they made the sheds. They were real warm and nice. So if Stepmother was short of kindlin' sometimes and if she was mad about anything, she'd go and break little pieces off of these dried faggots and bring them in, and Father got rather angry about that I remember once.

And he had money in a strongbox in the house to pay bills when they came around. Nobody heard about checks in them days. So if he didn't want to come in in his dirty feet, he'd say to Stepmother, "Here's the key. Go and get out whatever it is so I can pay for that horse," or pay for whatever. So she'd go and get it out for him.

And then one time later on she forgot to give him back the key. So when he wanted some more money, there wasn't any there at all. My, that sure did create a commotion in our house. She said it wasn't there, there was none there.

Well, then she let on she had burned those notes up. What she'd ever done with them nobody ever knew. They were bank notes. It went on and on for a long time, the commotion. They got lawyers and everything, but I don't know how it ever ended. It was still goin' on when I left home, I know that. I was so glad to get out of there.

She had a brother that was real crooked, and once in a while he'd come and stay there—her brother was a no-gooder, you know. And when he was gone the boys always missed their watches and missed their things that they had. And you couldn't say anything. It was wrong to accuse anybody of stealing anything. That was close to accusing and that was against the law. The fact was, the things were gone.

We were wheat farmers. That was what we did. That was our main thing, was wheat. We sold wheat all over England. A lot of our wheat was sent away. They bought brand new gunnysacks–they were beautifully made, you know. It was almost like they were starched, and the wheat, after it was gathered, was then put in stacks and stayed in stacks until the frosty weather come. That was when they thrashed it those days. And then they put it in the barn, loose, and then it sort of steamed off or dried off, and a little later on someone held sacks open, and someone shoveled it in. Each sack was weighed before it was sewed up.

We had to have a huge barn and a good floor, you see, for that, 'cause it was 'sposed to be rat-proof too, so rats couldn't get in and that. And how we harvested the wheat was another thing too, because we didn't have all the machinery in those days. So they did have a machine that just cut it and laid it in rows.

Then we had to collect it into bundles the size of a pillow that you would sleep on, and then make our own band out of the wheat by taking the two heads of wheat and twirling them and puttin' them around the middle of these bundles of wheat until you had eight. And then you went all the way up the row like that, doing eight, and eight, and eight, in clusters of eights. Eight bundles, you see. Then, when you come back down the row, you'd stand those up, you'd stand those up against each other, and the bottoms kept them from falling over.

So those were the things. We called that shocking it then. Then if it should rain, the rain came on the top and went right down to the bottom, and they weren't standing in the water. They'd just stay there till the sun shined and dried them all out again.

Then later on when that was over, then they were put in huge stacks. When they were put in huge stacks, then the

45

wheat was put more on the inside of the stack, and they hada' have an experienced stacker so that–it was just like havin' an experienced housecleaner–so that the stacks balanced. There were people like our neighbors' cousins or somebody like that that were stackers. And when they were stackers, then they held their job as a stacker. There wasn't anybody else. There wasn't any "I'm goin' to stack it today," and "I'm goin' to stack it tomorrow." They was the stacker, so that was that.

Then there were those that pitched it up to them, put it on the fork and put it up to them. They had to be careful they didn't shove it up there so they'd prick the guy's hands when they were takin' it off or anything.

The wheat was ripe about September, between the early and the middle. They had to have a good many suns on it, hot September suns, you know, between the end of August and September. Then, when the stacks were finished off, they had to be finished off like the roof of a house, so that they would shed the rain.

But if that night the stack was finished, then they had to put a canvas over it, because if the rain should get into it or the dew should get in other ways, the wheat would be mildewed and then the flour would be mildewed, see. My father had bags, like marble bags, with the string, like they used to have years ago, you know. And Father had so many samples to carry.

So then he went up into Cambridgeshire and showed his wheat to the market, and then they bought his wheat, see.

That was in Ely, and then Cambridge too, you know. So then they sold all the wheat that way. They'd balance the samples in their hand, because if it was good hard wheat, see, then that was what they wanted. Then they gave a price for them, and if the price was fine, then that was that.

Haying near Hockwold early in the 20th century

We always saved twelve sacks back for own family because we used about a sack a month, see, about a hundred pounds of flour a month for our bread. Then, when the wheat was all harvested and gone, then we got paid for the wheat, see, right away. But it never really got thrashed out much until the frosty weather came. That was the funny part of it. And the threshing machine would come and start right in. Then it was all hands to the pump—all the hired help that we had around there had to get back and help out with that. So that was that.

Then after that, of course, it was time to start fixin' up the land again for another year. Some of the land was dry enough where you could plough and seed it, and they got the manure out. They didn't have manure spreaders in those days, so they put the manure in little piles all the way up the land, and they'd come down with the wagon and put another row along there, so they could drive the wagon between those rows of manure. On a frosty day when there wasn't anything else much you could do–you couldn't dig or stuff like that–well, you just went with the fork and threw this manure out, scattered it, broadcast it. And then when they ploughed it, see, they plowed it under and then they put wheat in again.

Oh, but after the land was ploughed and harrowed–disked sometimes if there was too much sod, and then harrowed— then they come with a drill, and the drill was real wide like, and they put a whole sack of wheat in the drill, what they was goin' to plant. And then it was drawn by horses, and then someone had to walk behind the drill, which was me, and make sure that it was running out of all spouts. It ran in spouts into rows, you see.

And after that was over, someone else comes along with a harrow, and then they cross-harrowed it. They went that way, and then that covered the wheat all up, see. But the land had to be fairly dry; it couldn't be wet and sticky because that wouldn't cover up, see.

And of course after the wheat was in, you see, then we were troubled with too many birds that would scratch the wheat out. If the birds was bothering the seed, then you had to go along with blue vitriol and sprinkle that all the way along the rows there, and that would kill the birds, lots of them. Because otherwise they'd scratch out all your wheat–you wouldn't have any crop after all. Those English sparrows were terrible.

We made hingles. We took two little stakes, sticks of wood with about two yards of string on them, and then we took horsehair. We made snares out of horsehair, by taking a whole long horsehair and twirling it in our fingers. We made a noose. And then we stuck those stakes in the ground and we sprinkled feed all the way along where these little horsehair snares were, and the birds would put their heads in there to eat, and when they went to pull them out, this would snare up around their feathers and we could take them out.

It's quite interesting, because you don't have to kill the birds to get them. Like if you took a piece of string and you doubled it so the two ends was together, or even a piece of thread. And then you twirl it, and then it leaves a little eye at the top and then you put this bottom end through that little eye, and pull it. And then that makes a little snare. And then you tie the end of this string, the end of this horsehair on your string that's along there, see, and the stakes are in the ground, but it's close to the ground, so when the birds sticks their heads in to eat the feed and they go to get their heads back, this snares up around their feathers.

It doesn't kill them, so you can let 'em out if you don't want them. 'Spose you had some bad sparrows and you wanted to get rid of them or something. Well maybe you'd catch a little robin in there and you wouldn't want to get rid of him, or a hummingbird or somepin' like that—you wouldn't or hardly get a hummingbird 'cause they don't eat those things, or somepin' else, why then you can let them go.

Sparrows and blackbirds could go in pies. And larks. It would take a bird for each person, see. And those pies were almost like boiled pies. You make the suet pudding, or the suet crust, and put it in a bowl, like a lining of a bowl. Kind of make

Minnie Rose Lovgreen

a little hole there in the middle so the air can come up, you know, in them. Then you put these little birds in there, and a little onion. And then fill it about half full of water. And then you put a little salt and pepper, and you dip 'em in flour if you can, you know.

Anyways, if you had about ten or twelve people, you'd need at least ten or twelve birds. Now this was in a basin, you see, in a bowl. And then you stood the bowl on a cloth, like a big square diaper, we'll say. And then you tied the four corners up. And you plunged them into a thing of boiling water—it had to be boiling water—and keep boiling, And that would boil for about three hours or so.

So put them on after breakfast and they was done by lunchtime. You didn't have to worry about them. You built a turf fire, so that the water was boiling when you put them in. When you took them out, oh the smell of those was just delicious. We made rabbit pie the same way. And then once in a while they'd make a baked rabbit pie, but that was very seldom because it took a whole brick oven to heat for the rabbit pie—and you felt that if you heated an oven you had to fill it up, for economy. See, you didn't want to waste all the rest of that oven. So the bird pie was very delicious.

And then we also got the bird eggs. We were short of eggs, even though we raised our own grain. We had a few chickens running around there. No one had a proper chicken house. The chickens perched up in a tree or wherever they wanted to go, or sat up in the barn somewhere.

And then the bird eggs, we got the bird eggs. And if we had any, say about two cupfuls of bird eggs, that would make a good-sized custard. Stepmother would bake a custard with them, so when she was goin' to heat the oven, we all had a little custard. She'd beat the eggs up and then put some sugar with them and then fill the thing full of milk you know, and that was that.

They put a little egg cup in the middle of a deep apple pie or whatever they was making—they put a little egg cup upside down in the middle so that the pastry rested on that so that if the meat sank down or anything, it would still stand up in the middle because this egg cup held the pastry up. You could take an old cup with the handle off it, or anything like that, but it seemed like we didn't have no cups with no handles, so.

They had real nice china that was kept for the best. Some Staffordshire china. The cups was pretty. They were narrowed at the bottom and flared out slightly at the top, but they were more upright than some of these that flared out all the way. And then Stepmother had a tea tray. It would hold the teapot and about six or eight cups. And that was always stood in front of her at the table. And the teapot had a cozy over it–it was something that was quilted. So when you set down to eat, you don't keep gettin' up and gettin' somethin' else you forgot.

We had oval-shaped earthenware pans–there wasn't any aluminum in those days. Or we had enamel. And the enamel pans had a little edge on them, like a flower almost, so if you were making a pastry and goin' to bake it, you could put it over the edge of the little rim that was all the way around them, and you could flute them by just takin' your finger and go along like that.

We got the cheese from the grocer's, And they only go a very small little piece of cheese for a great big family, so people ate their bread all the way around till they come to the cheese and then they left the cheese till almost the last, because they said "the cheese is a sassy elf, digesting all but not itself." So they ate the cheese last.

We got what we called Red American cheese. Father liked cheese, and so we figured that he had the biggest responsibility and the hardest work and everything. If the boys went to cut a piece of cheese when Stepmother was out, they'd say, "Oh, don't eat all that cheese. Poor father paid seven pence for that," and so everybody cut a very small piece of cheese. There was a lot of friction.

We had a dairy, something like a little pantry on each side. Yes, we called it a dairy, because there was another one the other side of it that was called a pantry, partition between. You only went down two steps into that, it was like a little bit of a cellar. It was about as big as a pantry, with wide shelves. They had big milk pans, earthenware milk pans, that was just about as big around as a great big preserving kettle or somepin' like that. Now the morning's milk went in the pans on the left side. So the morning's milk would be skimmed off the next morning for cream, and then the calves would have the skim milk.

So these pans had to be washed up. And they rinsed the pans out and put that in with the calf milk too, so that nothing was wasted. There wasn't anything wasted. They sterilized the pans. They had kettles of boiling water on the stove, and they washed them with cold water first and then with the other. And it was my job always to get that water from off the bank, and I had to go down to the bank and lift up two buckets with a pair of yokes on my back and two chains, and bring that up like that and put it in a big barrel, so Stepmother never had to go and get water.

I had to get fifty pails on washday. And washday was on Monday. And then Stepmother washed the clothes with a washboard like that. But she didn't want to wash my clothes. She just couldn't think about what she had to do for the rest of the family. She had to wash the men's shirts and their underwear. When it come to my underwear, if I could get somewhere behind a corner and slip mine off and tuck it under there, then she wouldn't know it was under there, then she'd have to wash it 'cause it was in there. But she wouldn't let us wash it.

These clothes, afterwards, they hung them out on the line, you know. I don't think they ever wore out. Because you see these drying machines that we have now, they'll wear out our clothes. I've noticed it where I've gone, again and again, all that lint that comes off of things. I have clothes now, blouses that I've had for over four years that I wash out and hang up and they're just as good as new, and I know it's just the machines that wears them out. But back then we wore out our hands, you know, we wore out our hands tryin' to wash these clothes.

I've got three pails in my bathroom. And I couldn't do that if I wasn't living alone, 'cause I'd have to share the bathroom with someone else. Soon's I take my underwear or anything off, they go into a pail of water. And when I get time I rinse 'em out of that and into the next pail, then into the third pail, then hang 'em up in there, and I've always got clean clothes, any day. Just take them off whenever I want to.

53

But they had a corner in the room where they had built in a concrete or plaster big bowl shaped like an ice cream cone, and underneath that were little holes where they built a little fire under it. And they said it was all copper, that little thing that was in the corner there. It was all copper, and they had a wooden lid on the bowl, and then they stirred 'em down with a broomstick and rinsed them in water. So that was the washdays.

We wore dresses, mostly serge dresses. Then there was another thing, somepin' like gingham that would be for the summer months, but you only had two dresses. You had a winter one and a summer one. The gingham one was, they called 'em linsey, they was kind of a faded blue.

And then you wore a pinafore over them always. The pinafore was made of white with the gingham or anything like that. And sometimes when you were working outside, you took a gunnysack and cut that open and pinned that around you as you were working around in the garden or somepin' like that. If you were lime-washing or anything like that.

I don't think Stepmother—I never saw her sew dresses. I know she made our chemises out of what we called calico, but it was unbleached cotton. Chemises was like shirts with a drawstring, an undershirt. I don't think they had a sleeve in them. No, they didn't. They just, you could pull them over your head. They didn't have wool or nylon, or anything like that. You just pulled them over your head and they came down about, almost up to your knees. And then there was the underpants made of the same material.

I don't know whether somebody ever gave us those dresses.

or just where we got them, but I do know that the serge, you couldn't, shouldn't get any spots on them or anything, If you was goin' to school you had to be sure and wear a pinafore so that you kept your dress clean. Your dress was always clean.

Stepmother usually wore a skirt and a blouse to work around the place. And she must have had some kind of a jacket, I think. And she had a very pretty gray dress. They came almost down to your feet those days. And a tight bodice, you know how they wore, the tight bodice with a waistline. And she had a little row of fur all around the bottom of her dress. That was 'sposed to be a very pretty best dress. That was made of serge of some kind. Sometimes they got Scotch wool, but this was a very fine cloth anyways, and I can't remember whether those were leg o'mutton sleeves.

But she had very nice clothes, and she was particular about her clothes. And then I don't remember too much about her hats. But they almost all wore hats those days.

And of course my father always wore suits and a tie—but not to work in. They didn't wear overalls to work in, they wore cloth things. No one heard about jeans. They wore cloth pants to cut up for the rugs, you see.

And they were lined. They were wool, lined with unbleached cotton, I think, closely woven wool or cloth. They bought them. There was a place in Ely where they could buy the clothes, but they sure lasted a long time, you know.

If they had a hole, they had to have it patched. My brother, if he had a hole in his things–Stepmother didn't get time to mend none of the things–he would look around for the thread and find it. We called that cobbling it up. He would patch it with his things.

And we weren't allowed to sew, to use any needles or anything like that. She didn't want us to sew. She had a drawer that she locked up, and that was the middle drawer, in a chest of drawers. So he found a way, so that if he took out the top drawer and he put his hand underneath there, he could find the thread to sew his holes up with. He got the thread and got a match and wound quite a bit on his match, and we always called it his wind.

"We walked all along the road (*to church*). You didn't meet anyone, hardly ever. Little country road. We enjoyed walking. They were straight dirt roads without any gravel."

And he had a needle. And he always had that where he knew where it was, so if he had a hole in any of his things he'd cobble 'em up somehow.

Now my father hated raggy sleeves or anything like that, so if no one had time to mend his sleeves he'd take the scissors and trim all the frays off of 'em, you know. But his was mostly all cloth things.

And they wore waistcoats those days. I didn't hear too much about sweaters. They wore blue gingham shirts. Sometimes they were good material and sometimes they were the lightweight, cheap material.

At church they read little texts and stuff like that you know, and sang a few hymns, and that was all. And say a prayer, and that was all. But that was nice. And we had to walk 3 miles there and 3 miles back. The church was at Sedgefenn. That was a little village. We walked all along the road. You didn't meet anyone, hardly ever. Little country road. We enjoyed walking. They were straight dirt roads, without any gravel. You didn't find hardly any stones or rocks over there. In the wintertime they got real muddy. They stuck to your shoes. Horses and buggies could go along there, but they had great big wheel ruts where the wheels went and sunk in a long way.

And then the shoes. My uncle made us our shoes. We had shoes that laced up, like work boots. We had to go and get measured for a pair of shoes. He had to measure our feet for the shoes and then he made them out of leather. His name was Jim Enefer.

He lived in Hockwold. The whole thing, the whole street, just one big street, you know, with a church and a cemetery and a tavern and houses, somepin' like that. But it was called Hockwold cum Wilton. Well, we was in the fen, we was down the fen, down the moors. And we was five miles from anything–about five miles from Uncle Jim.

When the shoes was ready, we had to go try 'em on, but his measuring was very accurate, so they were just like according to measure, see. Our shoes were just like boys' shoes. They had leather laces in them. Father thought that our ankles always oughta' be protected. He thought that people would have weak ankles, so. And now we think that the ankles should have all the air they can get. And they laced up. When they got almost up to the top they had these little eyelets.

And then the straw mats outside the door, outside of our back door. We didn't have porches on the house, so there was a little platform there where you came in, you know. And that was all made of brick, that platform. So you couldn't clean your feet on brick, so I had to make mats out of straw. I braided the mats out of straw.

I've tried to remember how I did them. You took one piece of straw like this, see, you made it like that, flat down and straight, and then you take another piece under there and bring that over. And then you braid that a little bit, but then you bring this hand in but then you put another piece of straw. You keep on till you get a big round mat. And that was soft oat straw. That would last. It'd last and last, you know. We could shake 'em and rinse 'em off and everything else. They lasted.

They used a foot scraper all the time, too. That was built in each side of the step, each side of the door. Nobody went in the house with dirty feet. My father, when he was outside, would never come in the house with dirty feet. If he wanted something, he always asked them to give it to him.

We also made rugs to put in front of the fire. The rug could be about as wide as a door, and half as long. It was a pegged rug. You cut out little strips of (I've got a pegger, so I can show you sometime.)–you cut your pieces of cloth, and you did that when you wasn't doing anything else. Somebody give you an old pair of man's pants or jacket or somepin' like that, well, you'd cut it all up and make it into a rug when it was no good for anything else. Cut it into strips for pieces to make a rug and put them all into separate bags. Red in one, and gray in another.

You take a new gunnysack and cut it open. You can use one half side of it if you wanted to make a shorter rug, but if you wanted to make a long rug you leave it. And you don't wash it, you make sure that it's a clean one. You start with your little pieces of cloth (wool) and you use an instrument something like tweezers and you push it through there, grab ahold of the piece of cloth, bring it halfway through, and then by the time you pull that up, these two ends are up together. Then you go right along while you've got that folded like that, get that row done. Then you go another row right on the edge of that, same way.

If you wanted the edge all black, which is nice to have, then you want 3 rows of black. Then you come 'round here, do it the same way all around. Now if you have red, and you want to make a star design in the middle, you just do it that way, put that under and pull it halfway through, like that. You can use all your old material. Lay it down and pick it up any time you wanted. You see these rows are so close to each other that one holds the other up.

Minnie Rose Lovgreen

And they were very particular. They took some red flannel and they faced that whole back like that. And then that rug laid in front of the big fireplace that we had there. And then if you made more you had one each side of the table. You know, they didn't show the dirt. You could take 'em up and shake 'em out and put 'm down again.

We called them pegged rugs. We used an instrument, a pegger, to pull them through with. It was like a sharp awl, like a sharp nail. You put it in through the sack, and of course a gunnysack is porous so it goes in easy. And then you grab your strip and pull it halfway through, see, so the two ends are just as long as each other, see.

Well, my stepmother went out once someplace–she wanted to go someplace–and she didn't want to tell Father where she was gone. Of course, I didn't dare tell tales 'cause there'd be an argument or a fight, so I always did everything to keep peace. So she wanted to go someplace, and Father didn't want her ever to go and visit this particular woman, because she had red hair and she was a fast woman. Father called her a fast woman, and he didn't like any of us to mix up with fast people, so he didn't want her to go over, and so she had me row her over the river.

We had a boat there. And when you rowed over the river you were in Suffolk. When you were this side of the river, you was in Norfolk. So you just had to row over the river. So she said, "Will you row me over the river?" And then, "If you don't tell Father where I'm going—to Mrs. Sizer's"—she said, "I'll let you sit outside and work on your rug."

Well, I'd been making that rug for her as a surprise and (at first) she didn't know it. But when I had to go up a ladder, see— our little house had two stairways—there was one where the girls and Father and Stepmother went to bed—and then the other side was a regular ladder where my brothers all went to bed, so they never could get together and talk at night. And there was a wall, so if we wanted to say goodnight to them we could bang on the wall and say goodnight, but we couldn't get in each other's rooms, that's one sure thing. And they never went our way.

But I always had to go up and make their beds when they were gone out to work on the land. So when I went up to make their beds, Stepmother always said, "Be sure and look in among the blankets," to see if they'd taken any fleas up there from the yard, you know. So that way I could take a little bit longer. And lots of times I couldn't find any fleas, but once in a while there was, off of a dog or a cat or somepin' like that, you know. She didn't want them to increase, so she always told me to look for fleas—pick 'em up and drop 'em in a little can of kerosene or somepin' like that.

I thought, well, this is an idea where I can start my rug and I'll give her that for a present. I had no money and that was one thing I could give her for a present. So I started working on the rug, and the boys gave me their old pants and their old coats and I'd cut them all up, and each day I'd do two rows when I got up there.

But she began to be suspicious of me being up there so long. She'd call me and say, "Haven't you done them beds yet? What's takin' you so long up there?" I said I was looking to see if I could find any fleas. I'd scuffle my feet around once in a while, so she'd hear I wasn't asleep up there or anything like that.

She never could come up there because it was a ladder—she wasn't a climber. You had to go up a ladder, then crawl through a hole like you was goin' up in an attic. But this one time she kind of surprised me. She thought she'd venture up there and see what I really was doing, and she caught me makin' this rug. I told her I was making it for her.

She just couldn't get over me, because when I started doing anything she always took me wrong, like I was doing it for some benefit of my own, you know. So I was goin' to give her that for Christmas. I had no intention of wantin' a rug myself. I don't know whether she ever scolded herself for being mad at me over that or not, but I told her I was making it for her. She told me it was underhanded and this and that and the other, you know, and so on, and called me all kinds of names. I couldn't say anything back.

So then when she wanted to go over and visit Mrs. Sizer, she said, "Then I'll let you sit outside in the sun and work on your rug." And the rug was goin' to her anyway. So I set out there and did the rug. And then, of course, I had to watch out, for when she came up on the other side of the bank so then I could row over and get her. She couldn't trust herself to row.

But there wasn't anything. You got in the boat, and you had a long pole, and you pushed it one side and the other. It wasn't a very wide river, that they called the Brandon River, you know. And then there was a certain landing place, so when the boat was up there, then she could go and she could see this other lady.

Father didn't ever like those ginger-headed women. He didn't mix with 'em. And she couldn't come over to our place 'cause she had no boat. So I worked on the rug, and I think I eventually got the rug finished, but I don't remember if she ever gave me any flannel to line it with or not, but when they lined it with flannel, gee, they were just beautiful. You just could sit down on them and they were nice to walk on. They always looked nice—cozy and everything.

First time I climbed out the window to run away, they were arguing about me. One argued that I was fine, and the other argued that I wasn't any good. So anyways, I thought before the arguments got any worse I better get out, so I climbed out the window and ran away. I went about two or three miles up the bank, the riverbank, and I hid there under the brush or a little tree. I set there. I was tired.

Then my brother came on horseback and got me, my brother Sidney. He said he knew if I'd run away that would be the way I'd go. So he went up that way, and he found me settin' under this brush crying, so he got me and brought me home on horseback.

And then the next time I run away, I got a little further away that time. And then my oldest brother came and got me. He didn't have any horse, so I had to walk home. He kind of drove me home. I said, "I'd just as soon go and jump in the river."

He said, "You'd be afraid of getting wet. You'd better be getting home. I had to come a long way to find you this time." It was always near evening, near nighttime.

So I ran away three or four times when there was an argument in the house. I'd always climb out the window and climb down the wall and run away. They always had to come and get me, to look for me and find me. It was always before night, because it was always almost dark before they missed me. Then they'd come and find me. I knew I wasn't going to get a spanking when I got home or anything like that. Just get upstairs, get upstairs, without anything to eat, usually. Of course, I was terribly thin then.

Hockwold home of some Minnie Rose relatives. The girl (4th from the left) may be Minnie Rose's sister Mary.

Chapter Two

1899-1912

Leaving Home~Housemaid~Mother's Helper

~ *"...I ran away...when there was an argument...."*

~ *"Things always come into my head*
for doin' things at the right time."

Things always come into my head for doin' things at the right time. One day my brother Fred came outside and he said how was I getting along, and I said, not very good. I didn't like to be there. I didn't want to be at home any longer. I wanted to get away. I wondered if he would write to Mrs. Shelton and ask if she would write home to my stepmother and ask for me, because she'd already had my oldest sister and then my second oldest sister to work for her, and they had grown up and graduated from there and gone. They were mothers' helpers, and that was a "breaking-in" place, as we called it.

I said if she would write home and ask for me and say how badly they needed me, well, maybe Stepmother and Father would let me go. I was ten and a half or eleven then. And so my brother didn't say anything. He just took it all in.

And the next thing I knew, about two or three days later, there was a letter from this lady. So he had written, and he'd never let me know that he had written. I didn't even know that he listened. And she wrote and asked for me.

Then Stepmother said, "I'm sure Father won't let you go. You're no good anyway. They wouldn't keep you in the house 10 minutes."

I said, "Well, I could at least try." I always had something—we weren't allowed to talk back. So I said, "I could at least try. If I make some money I could send some home to help you to raise the other children"—that was, her children.

So she said, "Well, I'm sure he probably won't let you go."

Pretty soon he called me to come and help him feed hay to the calves. So I went out and was helping him, and he said, "Mother had a letter from Mrs. Shelton. She wants you to go and work for her."

And I said, "Oh, that would be nice, Father. I'd like that."

And he said, "Well, we can't let you go. There won't be anyone to harness up the horse for me when I have to go to town to get the groceries, and there won't be anyone to clean my shoes and do all the other work."

I said, "There's plenty of people to do the work, but they won't do it as long as I'm here, because they let me do it all, and they won't be worth their salt, as long as I stay around here. When I get away they'll have to do it. There won't be anyone else. They'll have to do it." And so on.

There was four younger and then another one coming, always another one coming. So I said to Father then, "If you don't let me go, I'll run away when I get to the stage where I can't stand it any longer, and the next time you won't find me."

Then I said, "Because the other times it hasn't been too hard to find me, but you won't find me the next time."

Then my father said I always had hitched up the horses for him, and harnessed them, and gotten them ready to go to town, and always polished the shoes—the family never went out without polished shoes those days, you know—people always looked more at the shoes than they did at the rest of them. Sometimes I'd have thirteen pair of shoes to clean, Saturday nights or Sunday mornings. You put blacking on and let it dry a little bit, and then you polished them with a brush, and they polished real nice.

So anyway, Father and Stepmother talked it over again. They had separate meetings–they never talked in front of me. So they talked it over again, and he said, "Well, buy her some clothes and let her go."

So they bought me then a dress, a jacket, and a hat. The dress was a serge dress with a little white braid around it. It flowed from the yoke, and I didn't like it because it flowed from the yoke. It was a stiff serge, and when the wind blew it made me look like a tumbler. I always felt as if I wanted a sash around it. So I went upstairs and found an old trunk up there, and I found a piece of blue satin. I tied that around me, and I forgot to take it off when I saw Stepmother, and she said, "Where did you get that from?"

"Oh," I said. "I found it."

She said, "You've been looking in my trunk." Right then it gave the game away. She knew that piece of satin wasn't no place else but only in her trunk. She wouldn't let me wear it. It did look funny around that, but it felt better on than it looked,

67

Minnie Rose Lovgreen

I'm sure. It was that dress flowing from the yoke like a princess style. And all that wind getting out there, and that white braid at the bottom, zoom, looked like I'd just blow away.

The hat was a real big straw hat with daisies. Not like Shasta daisies, but Marguerites we called them back then. And it had two little blue ribbons hanging down the back. And they got me a little three-quarter jacket with buttons down—blue serge or black or something like that.

Then before I left, I taught them how to hitch up the horses and all that, how to put the harness away and how to examine them. Before the horses went out, you had to go over all the straps and make sure there wasn't anything pinching them or scary when they was going—everything had to go smoothly.

So then they put me on the train and the people was to meet me the other end of the train. In those days we had no telephones and no way of letting them know, excepting my family had written a letter saying I'd be on a certain train, so they would meet the train. This was in Cambridgeshire. In a place called Ely.

The train ride was just wonderful. I don't think I remember ever being on a train, exceptin', see, when my own mother died when I was four. I had gone on a train with her to Wisbech once.

Well, the Sheltons met me and they took me up to their house and they said where was my suitcase, and I said well, I didn't have anything because Stepmother was going to send the rest of the things. And they supplied what they wanted you to wear in the house–they supplied house dresses–so all you had to do was put a dress over your others and you were dressed. Those clothes that you had on was to go to church in or wherever you went.

So anyway, I had a good talk with the lady, Mrs. Shelton, and she said she wanted me to go to church every Sunday with them, and to church in the evening, and I said that was agreeable, I would like that.

Well then, I went about my cleaning and my work. Sweep upstairs and that. They told me to sweep one room real good, make sure that I went in all corners. They thought most of the people would do the middle and would leave the corners, you know.

When I came down, Mrs. Shelton said, "Did you go in all the corners?"

I said, "Oh yes, I did."

So she said, "Well, did you find a button up there that belonged on this coat of mine?"

I said, "No, I didn't see a button. No, I didn't see no button."

Well then, they knew I didn't go in all the corners, because they'd put that button in there. So then that taught me to go in all the corners. And then they also taught me to always go out backwards after I'd cleaned up a room, to make sure I didn't leave a duster or a broom or anything laying around.

It was quite a good idea, you know, to walk out backwards. And I taught myself that (years later) when we had the dairy too, so we'd never leave shovels and things standing around the barn for the animals to fall over.

Well I got a little lonely that first week, and I was wondering if I could stick it out. But something happened. I had to eat my meals in a little tiny pantry. They gave me my oatmeal in this little pantry, you know, for me to eat alone. And there was a little window in the pantry.

Then every morning the little birds would come and set on my windowsill, so I'd hoist the window up and put a few crumbs out there for them. They come every morning when I was eating, those little birds did, and ate breakfast with me. They always seemed to know when I was going to eat, because they always came. Just a few crumbs of bread I'd give them. Almost nobody had toast them days. So those little birds kept me company.

So anyway we got along real good. And when the week was up they asked me, then it was washday, and I wasn't old enough to wash clothes.

I wasn't old enough to wash clothes, so they asked for my clothes to be washed, and I didn't have any. My uncle was supposed to bring them up, but my stepmother hadn't made any. Stepmother always made our underwear and our little calico chemises. And you had stockings with garters on.

Mrs. Shelton said, "Well, I can't let you go another week without having a change of clothes, so I'll go upstairs and cut some of mine down to fit you and you can go up now and change, and then we'll wash yours that you have." So that's how I got my clothes washed. It must have been a month before Uncle ever brought me up mine.

So they had a housekeeper there, and this housekeeper was Miss Carrington, and she was deformed–she had a humped back, you know. So she could live there so long as she'd keep house for them, like, and look after me, I 'spose, 'cause the lady

(Mrs. Shelton) was partly an invalid, you know.

And she (Miss Carrington) may have had some kind of income because she acted quite self-dependent. So she would get after me quite often, and I wasn't one who could take orders from two people very good, and I still can't, unless they're both pulling together. Lots of times I resented her interference, but she got so she learned not to interfere too much, so that worked out good for both of us.

So I stayed there. And they were strict vegetarians. It was a religion with them—they didn't believe in killing fish or anything that had to be killed. So most of their food was protein food. And their macaroni cheese was just almost out of this world when they made that. That was one dish that everybody just loved.

Their names were Edward Elbey Shelton and his wife, Frances Shelton. And then the other little lady was Marian Carrington. They had a beautiful, big two-story house like all the old English homes are, you know. It was just on the outskirts of Ely. It was far enough out, so you had to drive to the store in a little pony and cart.

I kind of looked after her, sort of like a nurse to her. I don't know what the lady was sick with, but she was taking a lot of medicines. She was delicate, had a delicate stomach. But she got better and she lived to be almost a hundred. They were vegetarians, her and her husband. And he was secretary-treasurer of a church in London.

My sisters got sassy when they worked for her, but I didn't get sassy, you see, because I knew that I didn't want to go home, and so I stayed with them then. But then they moved from Ely to Surrey, near London, you know. I went with them there and that's where we kept the goat.

I said, if she got a goat, I could milk it, and then she could have that goat milk. So I milked the goat to get her well and everything, and give her the goat milk in the morning at six o'clock in her bed. I took her the goat milk right warm from the goat in the morning up to her room, and then she drank that, a glass of it with a straw, you know.

And then she worked in her greenhouse, and then at ten o'clock another glass of goat's milk, and at lunchtime again, see. And she got real better, because otherways fifteen doctors had given her up to die, you know.

And then the goat got bred. Maybe she got loose one day and went over where there was a billy goat, but of course no one knew she was pregnant.

Later on, Mrs. Shelton said that if she had a little pony and cart she could drive to the store. So I said that if she got a little pony my father would break it in for her, and she could have a little cart made if that's what she wanted. Then they got a little Shetland pony and my father broke the little pony in for them.

The little pony's name was Bessie, and she was a little Welsh pony. She was bigger than one of those tiny ponies that the children ride. Father broke her in, and then he brought her out to me and told me all the tricks, you know, with her, like if she was sensitive about any one particular thing.

They called it a trap. You didn't get in the sides-you opened a door and got in the back–and the seats was each side, they faced each other, so she could take her friends to the store to do their shopping. And then she sat up in the front, in one of the side seats, but she had the reins and she did the driving, so she was quite happy.

And it was just wonderful for me, because I would have less housework to do and more outside work.

So when I went to catch Bessie, I always took a little pan of oats along. And then she knew what it meant. You know, we never started a thing and then changed our minds about something. It was always continuing what we were doing.

So she knew the tricks, and so we got her to the cart, and then I stood and took care of her till they came out, kept her mane all brushed down, you know—she had a nice long mane. And the forelock, sometimes I'd braid them up, you know.

Later on, well, this lady did very good, and this one morning they had two great big gates that enclosed their yard, iron gates, and I was closing the gate after I'd started them off to the store. And the gate came off the hinge, knocked me down, and I was buried under the gate.

They come back and picked me up, took me in, and laid me on the couch, and if I was knocked out I came to anyway, so they never had to have the doctor, so everything was all right.

You see, Mr. Shelton didn't know a thing about ponies, and I don't think he ever rode in the cart either. And then I hooked it up and harnessed it thoroughly, you know, so she'd drive to the store to buy her groceries and things like that. She'd get in the back, you see. It had seats each side, so if she took friends with her they'd sit facing each other, so they could talk while they were riding, you know.

The little cart was a banana color. It was real attractive, beautifully polished. That was the only way of getting around.

Minnie Rose Lovgreen

They called it a pony and trap. It was a little cart that was made an oval shape, so that instead of getting' up on a stair and jumpin' in like we do on our cars, like we do these days, it opened at the back and you got in at the back and there were seats each side, you see.

So then, after I got them started, you know, to get the groceries, why then I'd do up some housework and do a few things like that. And then they'd come back, and then we had dinner and then I unharnessed the pony for them, you know, and put the pony away again. It was pretty good-natured, but you just had to keep it good-natured by being regular with the feeding, and if you weren't goin' to work it, then don't give it too many oats, you know–give it more roughage, like more vegetables and stuff like that.

But if you were going to work it, why give it a little more oats and that'd give it a little more strength. Give 'em time to eat the oats. So I did that. My father broke in horses for her and told me exactly the little tricks to know, so. And if she was like, if she acted up, and didn't want to be caught, well, you took a little pan of oats and called her with the oats, you know. And then you grabbed her. When she knew that you had her, well she didn't try to argue.

Well, they say a horse knows its owner, you know. So you treat it the same way all the time. And no one else ever handled it but me and her, see. The pony, she was Welsh, Welsh and something else. She wasn't a real big horse, but wasn't one of those tiny little Welsh ponies. She could take five people in the cart, anyway.

And then they had one son. His name was Percy. He was the one, he wrote to me after he got to Canada. He left England, and after he got through college he went to Canada. He went to Saskatchewan or Regina, or somewhere in there.

And then he wrote to me, and he said, "If my folks ask you to stay there a long time, and then if your brothers ever ask you to come to Canada, accept your brothers' advice, because it doesn't do to stay in one place too long or be tied to a person's apron strings."

He said, "Even though I don't want to interfere with your way of living, if my parents want you to stay, don't let yourself get married to the place, because it's educating to get around." Well, he knew I hadn't been to school at all. And he was older than I was.

You know, I was so ambitious for more education and more makin' progress around home there, around in England, that I didn't, I didn't think anybody'd ever attach me to come to Canada at that time, so I didn't pay too much attention to it.

Whenever she took both of us in the cart, why him and I would always get out and push the cart. We walked behind when they were goin' uphill, to push the cart, so it wasn't too hard for the pony. And it was so funny, you know. He was awfully considerate. He'd got through college and I would probably be only about thirteen or fourteen. And then he sent me a big bottle of perfume.

Anyway, he was a strict vegetarian and they were because they'd signed a pledge that they wouldn't hurt or kill any living thing that creeped on the earth because God had made these things, and there was enough food growing for human consumption rather than for people to have to kill them poor animals to eat them to exist. So he'd signed that pledge, so he was goin' to always be a vegetarian just like his parents was.

But anyway, he got to those different parts of Canada, and he was a reporter for the paper, see, so whenever he went to big meetings and that, he couldn't get enough to eat, so he had to learn to eat meat. That was what was called breakin' the pledge.

Then some time later, he thought he would study law and become a barrister. So he studied law, and he went through that, and later on he met a girl and he got married. They had one child, little Alfie I think they called her, and later on they had another little girl. They sent a picture of his wife. She was a very plain lookin' nice girl.

I finally got my bearings and got so I could write. Whenever he'd write to me he always typed, see, 'cause he thought maybe I hadn't been to school much. I could read his handwriting, and anyway, those people that do a lot of typing in England, they've got the funniest little handwriting you ever saw. They don't write distinct at all. I don't see how the postman can ever read it.

I remember him mailing a letter for me once in England and looking at the writing and saying, "My goodness, poor mailman. I'll be sorry for him if he ever gets that to the right place. I can't hardly read it myself. Well, see, that was my first letter I'd written and I couldn't hardly write the address. Anyway, it got there, where it was goin' to go.

So when he told me that, it always registered with me. He said how was he ever goin' to read that, where it had to go.

So I always remembered then I'd have to practice on handwriting.

So after he got all through being a barrister, you know, then he said he didn't realize there was so much crookedness went with it in Canada, so then he dropped the law. He just couldn't allow himself to continue that, so he went back to being a reporter for the newspaper.

* * *

So (years later) when I went to Vancouver, and I understood he was goin' to be in Vancouver, I thought it'd be nice to meet his wife and the children after those many years, see, 'cause he wrote and told me when his father died. He wrote and told me that he attributed his mother's long life and also his father's long life to the food, 'cause they lived to be almost a hundred. He believed it was stayin' away from meat.

Well anyway, when he got in Canada they ate a lot of beans, and some eggs and cheese, and a lot of parsley and stuff like that, and macaroni, of course. They do it up and make it look like a roast chicken, with macaroni you know in the legs and stuff like that. There's an awful lot of work to the vegetarian meals.

See, his father had a partner when he was in Ely and they had a stationary store. So the partner had a daughter called Reve (pronounced Reevee) and she was in Canada at that time, and her husband was the organist of Christ Church in Vancouver. He was a wonderful organist, he was, used to be the organist in the cathedral in Ely, in Cambridgeshire, and his name was Chubb. And he finally wanted more money like a lot of them did, you know. But his wife Reve, she used to have fits occasionally.

Almost nobody thought there was any cure for them, and they just let 'em go and they thought they'd outgrow 'em, like stuttering and any other thing. Now we work on 'em, but there they didn't. Years later, in Canada, I saw Reve and her two boys. She had two boys, see.

Then I also saw this little girl of Percy's and she was mentally deficient some way or other, too. She'd run back and forth again to the door, and slap her hands on the door and keep doing it repeatedly, and at first I thought it was a game, but then, after, Percy's wife said, well, she wasn't quite right. And then I never did get to see Percy either, because he was away on some newspaper job.

But when I saw Reve, though, she said, "Oh, my!" She hadn't seen me since I was just a little girl working for her friend's mother, you know. "Oh my," she said. "I can't get over it, Minnie. You've grown up and you're pretty." And she said, "You're pretty," see, because we always took care of ourselves.

Anyways, I always had a very good complexion, and so I grew up pretty. My hair was jet black. They called me black head when they wanted to call me names. And I had a very rosy complexion.

So anyway, then I didn't see too much more of them. And then, quite some time later, Mr. Chubb died and then I wrote back to her again and said I was sorry that she'd lost her husband. And she wrote a real nice letter back to me. Then she was eighty years old.

Well, Percy. Eventually him and his wife, they returned to England. When I was back in England (much later), I thought it would have been fun to look him up, you know, but I'm almost sure that he was gone by that time. He might have been and he might not.

I tried all over. There's what they call a red book in England, and you can search for people, where they are, but I never did find him. I'd like to have found him, though. I'd like to have seen him after all those years. It didn't matter what his parents had, see, or where they were. They weren't too much money people, but still he always wanted to be on his own.

* * *

Well, I worked there for the Sheltons about five years, and then I decided I wanted to go someplace else. I'd learn more things. I thought I wasn't learning enough then.

I went to another place, and that place was all right for a while. Then that was where the lady said she thought I was too young to be a cook. So she let me go then. She give me a reference anyway. They all give you a reference. That's one thing they can do for you. If they give you a reference, you were all set, see, and if you didn't have any reference, you wouldn't get hired, see, and that was that. They wouldn't believe you.

So I was there for a while. Then I left that place, and I got another place where this girl was cleaning the stairway and this man tried to make love to her, and the lady didn't stick up for the girl, and didn't do anything about it. And I left there then, and I didn't know where to go then. My position was cooking. I stuck to cooking because I knew they always wanted a cook, whatever else they didn't want.

79

So then I looked for another place and couldn't find anything, and I went to this one place where the little girl said, "I think we won't like you, because you put bones in the cakes. Mother said she didn't think you was goin' to be a very good cook because you put bones in the cakes."

And I said, "What cakes? I never made any cakes."

She said, "Yes you did. In the fishcakes."

And I said, "Oh, I'm sorry about that. I didn't know I left any bones in."

So I thought, well. And that night the man came home and he sounded like Barnacle Bill the Sailor, and I was terribly frightened. I wasn't very old. I think I was about fifteen to sixteen then, or about that.

So when he came home, I got out of my bed and I moved my dresser and everything in front of the door so he couldn't get in my room without me hearing him come in. And then I don't know what I would have done if he'd come in, 'cause he was a great husky man.

So the next morning, I got up and everything was quiet and I served the breakfast to them. I served the breakfast, I picked up my suitcase, my little overnight bag, and away I went. No reference from that place. I had to tell my own reference the next place I went.

I went to the manager of the bank. I went to the bank and I asked them if they knew of anything. I thought maybe the bank manager knew of somebody I could work for.

I don't know how I thought of that. Things always come into my head for doin' things at the right time. Nobody said, "Don't go there because they got too many children."

So I went to the bank then, and I thought, well, I'd ask the bank manager if he knows a place, and he said, yes, his sister needed somebody pretty bad.

I said I had references from two or three people, but I said this last one I didn't stop. And he said, "What'd you leave there for?"

So he said, "I can get you a place. My sister needs somebody pretty bad, and I can get you a place where you won't have to be afraid of anybody." So he asked me if I'd go on the train, and I said, oh yes, I didn't mind which way I went.

So he said, "All right. I'll put you on the train and I'll go get your trunk and send it along"—everybody had trunks them days. And that was in Dorsetshire, so I had to go a long way on the train. So he said, "I'll put you on the train, and I'll ship your trunk and everything for you. I'll see to it that it gets there." So he did, and I stayed with them right until the time that I came to Canada.

And they went away one year, and they said that I could either go with them or stay with the people in the house, or go home to my parents. And I said oh, I didn't want to go home to my parents, I'd go with them.

So they went to Wales, and I had a chance to go and see Wales that time. They went to Cardiff. I liked it very much. There was all those old castles there, you know. There was another maid there besides me, and we went around together at night when we had time, and looked at the old castles, and we got dinner through early, and we always went to walk somewhere, you know.

She was a Catholic and I wasn't. So when it was Sunday we

had to go to church, you know. They wouldn't have you if you didn't go to some kind of a church. So I said, "Well, I'll go to the Welch church.

So I went to the Welsh church and everything was in Welsh that was there, so I didn't understand the language. I come out—I laughed so much I had to come out—I didn't want to stay in there. So then I connected up with her again, and we went home and got the lunches, and then we could go for a walk wherever we wanted. It was really a nice life.

And then the next year, when these people was goin' to go away, they said I couldn't go with them, because they had to go where there wasn't anyone allowed exceptin' just them. There wasn't any room for any maids. So I said, "All right."

They were both schoolteachers. So I thought, well, I'll stay with the people in the house. So I stayed with the people in the house. Well, first of all, a lady there in the house said, "We'd like to take you to Egypt with us." She didn't have any right to take me away from the people that owned the house, because, you see, I belonged to them really. I was really hired out by them, and they kind of rented me with the house, so I was for rent then for a while. Then the lady said, "Would you go to Egypt with me?"

And I said, "Well, I think I would."

She said, "We'll pay you good when you're there." She said, "My son has enjoyed your cooking so much that since you've been here he gained weight." He was tubercular. And he was about twenty-seven years old. And she said, "I won't have to change cooks, and it'll be just wonderful to have you with us."

I said yes, I'd go.

Then, next day in the mail there came a letter from my brother to say would I go to Canada with him.

Chapter Three

1912-1917

Canada~Work~World War I

~ *"I was all looking ahead."*

~ *"The iceberg stood up like a three-cornered sheet."*

~ *"If you were choicy about what you wanted to do,*
then you better not come."

~ *"I can see the beauty of children now, but I didn't then."*

I went and told her that I was sorry. I couldn't keep my promise. I couldn't go with her, because I was goin' to go with my brother to Canada.

She said that wasn't right because Canada was an uncivilized place, and she called it all kinds of names and everything like that. She couldn't get me, though, anyway. Well anyway, by the time those people came back I was gone. And I never did write to them because I couldn't write very well. I wonder what they ever thought of me. I was gone. And they'd have to get someone else. They were particular who they got. They wanted to get someone who didn't live in the same town as they did–someone who was from far away so they wouldn't have too many friends, and stuff like that.

But I'd done a good job for them. I did everything they told me to. Also they'd done a good job for me, because they taught me about cooking and give me plenty of time to learn it and practice it, and everything like that.

I had learned to cook and read and write and sew. And I went back to see those same people I'd first worked for, the Sheltons, that was in Ely, before I went away, to say goodbye. And I stayed all night there. And they went and bought me a beautiful rug, a traveling rug, so I wouldn't be cold.

They admired me for wantin' to go to another country, because they said that if my older sister hada' done that she would have made something of herself. They said there was nothing there (in England) for her (Minnie's sister). If they go out to another country, they can make something of theirselves.

I had dark hair and it was kinda' straggly, but we had to do our hair up–you know. We had to always do our hair up–we couldn't have it hangin' around. There wasn't one hair out of place. You had to brush it up and pin it back somehow or other.

'Course in those days you wore little white lace caps, you know, to be in the house, and uniform dresses and stuff like that, that they supplied for you. A black dress in the afternoon with white cuffs and collar, and a white apron, if you were goin' to wait table. And you'd wear cooks' clothes, you know, down in the basement.

I just had my own idea about dress. I wanted all black or all white. I didn't want no gaudy colors, but that was always admired that little fur hat. They had little fur hats, you know. They were makin' fur hats.

I had to have my trunk made for comin' to Canada. They made it with basketwork inside, and then covered it with a kind of a leatherette. And they had a key with it, and I've still got my trunk. And a hat rack inside, you know, for your hats. And little wheels, castors, on it, you know. I had it made at Whitney's in London. They specialized in making trunks. I think it cost one English pound or somepin' like that.

So that way I had that and just a suitcase, and that was all I had. But the trunk got more bashed up coming on the train and on the boat than anyplace. It was just bashed up, you know. It was damaged quite a bit. It didn't look new looking. And I had my initials put on it–M.R.E. It's still on there–Minnie Rose Enefer. So that was the story of that.

In that trunk I packed all the things I'd want to use. Woolen underwear. They said we should have flannels, you know, so woolen underwear. A dress and a coat and a hat. And not too many other things. I'm sure my trunk was about full. I probably had a raincoat in there. They said it would rain a lot, but I don't think it rained any more in Canada than it did anywhere else. My clothes were mostly black, or dark colors. I remember my hat was black. But I did have that little fur hat that I traveled in. A little fur hat. Then I had that on my head.

When we got on the ship, it was a great big ship (*Note: Minnie Rose and her brother had booked passage on the* Titanic, *but when its sailing was delayed, they changed their tickets for the earlier sailing of the* Megantic *on March 30, 1912*), of course, and thousands of people on there, I don't know how many.

Anyway, they were all nationalities—Chinese and Japanese and Hindus with turbans on that we'd never seen before, that kind of scared you, all talkin' away in different languages.

Minnie Rose sailed on RMS *Megantic* from Liverpool on March 30, 1912, bound for Montreal.

I was all lookin' ahead–my mind was all lookin' ahead. And I'm sure the others were, too, but they were all sick on the boat coming over. Kinda' surprised me, but my brother and his wife and my cousin, they were all bedridden all the way over because they were seasick, and I didn't get seasick. So I went up on deck and looked around and mixed up a little bit with other people, but not too much, and found somebody to talk to when I was alone. And then when it was dinnertime, I didn't eat all the stews and hashes that they had. I just ate toast and marmalade, 'cause that would go down good, and that didn't make me feel sick. When I saw how sick they were, I didn't want to get sick like they were. The stewardess was down there cleanin' up after them all the time.

Minnie Rose Lovgreen

It was just bunk beds. See, we traveled third class. My sister and I had the two lower bunks, and two other women had the upper bunks.

Third-class passengers in good health were issued inspection cards permitting them to board. The picture shows Minnie Rose in 1912, the year she immigrated to Canada.

They all had traveling sickness. And so they were sick all the way over. They never came out of their bunks once. So I thought the poor things must need something solid to eat, so I took them down some of those hard ship biscuits, what they call Sailor Boy now if you buy one. And it seemed to hit the spot with them, they liked those. They could eat those. They were really thin like a soda cracker, only they didn't have any salt on them, I don't think.

When we came closer to Canada, it was Good Friday on the boat, Good Friday then, and we saw a big iceberg sticking up, and we thought sure the boat was going to hit the iceberg. At that time we didn't know anything yet about the *Titanic* sinking, see. So they steered away till they got away from the icebergs. The iceberg stood up like a three-cornered sheet, point down, and sticking up a point up into the air, and then two points out. And that was how the icebergs was. They're huge. You can't imagine. Every time water splashed up against the iceberg, seems like it would freeze more and more and more. And we thought sure the boat was goin' to hit those icebergs. But it didn't, anyway. They managed to steer away from them.

Then we got to Montreal and we went from there to Chicago. We found that was a windy city. We didn't know anything about the wind, but it was really windy and cold there. We went to Chicago on the train, and then we had to change trains there somewhere.

We took another train then to Vancouver, B.C. The country looked different, because we hadn't seen wooden houses before, and the houses were all wood. We'd seen houses of brick and stone. We hadn't seen all those little wooden houses. And my sister-in-law kept saying, "I won't have to live in one of them little wooden houses, will I?"

And her husband says, "No, no, you won't have to live in one of them." Well, that was all what they had, was wooden houses.

Canada especially looked like a slum then, you know, because it wasn't built up like it is now. There was people standing on corners talking it over and looking discouraged, because there wasn't much work, and people were sleeping on the floor in the City Hall, where they didn't have no place to go and sleep, a lot of the immigrants, you know. And so on.

Minnie Rose Lovgreen

Yes, it looked very junky and the street cars was poor. It was really miserable, you see, when we got into Vancouver, B.C. We went to an apartment house. And we had to wait there until the people that slept all night got up, so we could go to bed and sleep for a little while and then go down to my brother's. We still had to wait till they got those people up and then made the beds over again to let us go to bed for two or three hours, and then we got up and went down to my brother's place. We didn't get anything to eat till we got down to their place.

Well, then we went over to my brother's place and they had a cake. They opened a little box and they had a cake coming out with frosting on it. We only saw cake with frosting on it at Christmas in England. We were quite surprised. We thought, well, we must be in a rich country if we can have cake with frosting on it right now. It was a layer cake, with frosting on top and jam in the middle, I think. It was a great big layer cake.

So then when we got into Canada, you see, we stayed a few days with my brother and then we started huntin' jobs right away. My brother Alfred remembered that we had to hurry up and find a job. So he was looking around, checking the papers and looking around to see if he could find a job sweeping the streets at night or emptying the garbage. So he got a job, he got one of those jobs, and then my cousin got another job, the same thing. My cousin's name was Alfie, too.

So then first thing they thought about was buying a little piece of land and building a little shack on it, so that they could invite their parents to come over from England. They thought it was such a wonderful place and a golden opportunity for people. So that was what he did, my cousin. He bought a little piece of land and fixed it up—a little corner lot, you know—and they built a little temporary frame house.

And then I got a job in a private house. I got a job almost the next day. I knew I would if I looked in the newspaper, and then I had references from England.

But before I got a job, I got sick. I got real sick. I wasn't sick on the boat coming over, but I got real sick then, just the same as they had it on the boat, only I was completely out of my head, and I told them not to invite anybody in to see me, just let me alone and let me stay there. So they called the doctor, and the doctor said that if I had let myself be sick on the boat, then I wouldn't have had that sickness right then. I held back, see. It lasted three or four days, and he gave me some stuff and snapped me out of it, whatever doctor he was.

I'll never forget that. My head was all stuffy, I couldn't even see straight, and I didn't believe, you know, that I was ever goin' to get better. I just said leave me alone and just stay out of the room and don't let nobody come and see me. There was no after- effects from it. It was just like I should have had on the boat and didn't have it. They were all better of theirs. They got all better of their sickness.

So anyway, then I went down to look for a job and I found a job with a Mrs. Smith. They had two sons and they were goin' to school. So I got a house-mother's job there, with the children, and also helping to clean up her house and stuff like that.

I got that job through the paper, through the ads in the paper, "Help Wanted, Situations Wanted," see. It wasn't hard to get a job. You told 'em you was just fresh out from England, you know, and that you'd be willing to do anything they wanted you to, and you'd work at the price they wanted you to work at. I think the price might have been about twenty-five dollars a month. I think it was somethin' like that. They were very happy to have you.

I remember on one instance her curtains looked like they needed washing. They were sash curtains made of pongee. They were almost like they have in restaurants, you know, just halfway up the window. She said, "Oh my, those curtains are so terrible. I wish I had time to wash 'em but I don't have time, I have to go out and take my driver's lessons."

She was goin' to learn to drive a car. So when she was gone I thought, well, I'll take 'em down and wash 'em, so I took 'em down and washed 'em and got 'em dry and got 'em up again before she came home. I think I must of wrapped 'em up in towels, and I ironed 'em somehow or other. You don't iron pongee very much. I ironed them, but I ironed them crooked.

So when she came in I said, "Well, you won't have to worry about the curtains any more. I've washed the curtains and got 'em back up again."

And she said, "They're all crooked, you've got 'em all crooked." And I looked at 'em then and I could see they were crooked. I couldn't see they were crooked before without she told me they were crooked. They weren't squared out like they shoulda' been. There wasn't any lace or anything on them, but they just hung any old way.

She was goin' out again to another lesson, so when she was gone again I took 'em down and did 'em all over again. And that time I ironed them properly. She looked at the curtains when she came back, and I said, "Well, I did 'em all over again, so I hope this time that they look all right. I think they do."

She said, "You devil!" She meant to say that I was determined to do a thing and she'd never seen anyone like it—"You devil!" She was pleased. Nobody took 'em down any more. They were fine.

I stayed there for a while until I began to be dissatisfied with the job. The boys were gettin' a little older where they could get up on the counter and stand up on the counter and go in cupboards, and I'd never seen anything like that in England. We'd never seen anybody raid refrigerators or go up in cupboards and look for raisins and look for things like that, so I thought well, I better look for something else.

I don't know where I got the courage from, but I had it anyway, so I started lookin' in the paper and I found where someone else wanted someone for cooking. So I thought, well, I think I've done quite a bit of cooking so I can take this cooking job.

So I did. I went over there and took that job. This lady was very happy to have me. And she questioned me. Her name was Thompson. And she had four or five children, I don't know which, but anyway the children weren't allowed to have as much freedom as they do nowadays. So they all had a nurse leadin' them by the hand, you know.

And then the folks all come from England. In the fall of the same year they came out, a whole bunch of them, all relatives. I'd knew 'em in England, you know—they were all cousins and aunts and uncles and that. After all, it was the same year that we came out, the fall of the same year. And my father and stepmother came at the same time. They couldn't stand to be in England after we left. They said that if everybody kept coming over here, and nobody went back, that there must be something fascinating about it.

So we went to watch, to meet this train, every night. We never knew when the train was coming in. There was no lineup on them or no nothing modern about it. So we finally found this place and the train came in and the depot doors opened, great big wide gates, and we saw all those relatives and children, thirty-three of them, come flockin' through there. And they all went to different places. My cousin let them some of them come down to his place, where he'd fixed a place for them.

And so I was there for quite a while, and they didn't have anyone else, and the lady began to say that she wished she had someone that would take care of the children, so she better put another ad in the paper, so then she'd have two people in the house. So she put another ad in the paper.

And Celine answered the ad, appeared at the door, and that's how I met her. I answered the door and she said, "Is Mrs. Thompson in?"

And I said, "No. She will be in after a while. Would you come in and wait?"

She said, "I looking for job." She couldn't talk very much, you know. "I looking for job. Job still open?"

And I said, "Oh yes, the job's still open." So I talked to her for a little while, and I didn't know too much about her, but her name was Celine Trasscheart. She had come over from Belgium with some people that went to Vernon, B.C. These people had paid their girls' fare over. There was two girls, two maids, and they told them that if they escaped or run away to get another job, that they would get even with them. So they were supposed to be pinned down to them, you see.

But the chauffeur they had there said, "Don't pay attention to that. If you want another job, you get another job." Because they had to go way over in the field and haul the water up to the house. They had no modern conveniences in Mt. Vernon, B.C. They had to haul the water in, probably with yokes on their shoulders, I don't know. But anyways there was a lot of hard, slaving work to do there, and they thought those girls would be willing to do it. But they got wise to themselves and didn't want to. So I think they both left. I think the chauffeur helped to smuggle them out.

Celine's hardest job was to understand what you said to her and speak the language, because, you see, those people that she came out with was from Belgium.

So then the lady of the house came in, and she accepted her. She asked her if she'd take the children to the beach every day in the afternoon, and she said she would, and stuff like that. But she really didn't like the job, because she really didn't like to take the children to the beach. She wasn't a children's person. She said she'd change jobs with me, but I said no, I was goin' to have to keep my job. I think my job paid a little bit more.

However, she said to somebody—I don't know how she said it, how I got to hear of it—that the cook was very nice–I was the cook. So I thought, well, if she thinks I'm nice, then maybe I can make a good friend of her. So, in the evening she had to set the table in the other room after the children got all settled, for their sleeping quarters and everything—she had to set the table, so—put everything on the table that she thought. So I'd say, "Well, have you got everything on the table?

"I don't know." She would always say, "I don't know."

So I said, "Well, we must look. No," I said. "You haven't got the water glasses on. You haven't got the serviettes on"—that was the napkins. They all had a ring for their serviettes those days, a little ring to show which was theirs. The serviettes were linen, you know. They weren't paper ones.

So after a few things, she said, "Sacrustee!" (sacre bleu?). That was a Belgian word, Sacrustee, like it seems–"Oh, my goodness! I would like better to have your job."

And I said, "No, I don't want to give up my job."

So she stayed there for quite a little while. And then there was a chauffeur next door to us that was working for somebody else, and she got acquainted with him, I don't know how. She was attractive, you know, she was very attractive. She had a way of attracting men as well as women. Men, especially. And so she talked to this chauffeur and he said, "Oh, you find another job and I'll help you to move."

So we looked in the paper every night, every night we looked in the paper, to see if she could find another job. Well, she said she wanted a job so that, when I had a day off, she'd have a day off, too, so we could go out together. Because she didn't have anyone else to go out with, see, and we could go down and see my parents, and everything like that. Of course then my parents hadn't arrived yet. But when they did arrive, then she still figured that she wanted a place where she could go down and see them.

She couldn't write the English language, and we didn't have any chairs in our bedroom, and we both shared the same bed, so we had to kneel down alongside the bed and write letters. So she wanted me to teach her how to write, and to spell the English words.

So she then went down with me to see my father, my parents, and she liked them very much and felt very much at home. A friend with her once was a friend always. So we went down, and when we came back from there she said, "I want to write and thank them for that good time we had."

"So I said, "Well all right, we'll do that now." So we got on our knees alongside the bed, and I was teachin' her how to spell this and how to spell that. I had no education myself, but here I was teaching her.

And so then I said, "Well, that's nice now. I've got a stamp so we can mail these tomorrow." She said no, she'd like to say some more about that good time we had down there, the people that she met and how she liked them, and she couldn't find the words to say for them. So we had to hatch up a few more words then, and finally we got it. Finally we got it so that we could mail the letter, and that was satisfactory.

And then she looked in the paper and she saw this other job. So we went every night after we got done and walked along the sidewalk to see how big the house was from the outside. And whenever she saw a house with too many windows she didn't want that because she knew she'd have to clean all them windows. You see, she had her eyes open for everything. No, she didn't want that. And there was too many steps up. No, she wouldn't take that job.

So we come across another one , a Mrs. Cline, so she said, "I think I'd like to see that house. That house don't look too big and too hard to clean." She knew if she had to do all that work it was going to be kinda' hard, so.

Celine was tall and real slender, flat-chested, real flat-chested, and she always said she wished she could develop a bust like other people had. She didn't see why she had to be so flat-chested. And we found out she could sew so good, so she made all my clothes. She made my suits and made all my clothes. She could measure with her hands. She'd stretch her hands out and measure from her thumb to her little finger, and go over on the next, and see how many she had over to make a yard, and so on.

So she made me a corduroy suit with a Norfolk style, with a belt around it and buttons down it, you know. And then she made me a little hat to go with it, a little brown Tam o' Shanter. And boy, I really felt stunning in that. She thought I looked real good—"Oh, you look so different, so different in this, you know." The suit was brown, penny brown. Penny brown suited me them days. It worked out pretty good. It was all corduroy and it was corduroy velvet, and it didn't wrinkle much when you set on it, either.

She made her own clothes too. She learned in Belgium. She was just naturally gifted. She didn't have a sewing machine that was a treadle. She had one that you turn by your hand, you know, yes, 'cause we all had them them days. I had one. I bought one when I was in England. Then I left it there with my brother, because it was too hard for me to bring it over here. Don't know what happened to it now anyway, because my brother passed away, and his wife passed away, so it was one of those things that got sold.

I wore a brown petticoat and a white petticoat over it. And she made me a coat, then. It was getting wintertime so she was goin' to make me a coat. So she went and bought me a remnant. She was sure that she could get a coat out of that remnant. She put a piece in the sleeve, underneath it. I said I didn't mind having a piece in the sleeve, underneath it. That wouldn't show where it was. So she bought the most beautiful material then in this remnant. To make me a coat.

So she had that, and she said, "You're going to wear that coat tomorrow." I didn't see how I could wear that coat tomorrow. She didn't finish off the seams or anything, but she stuck it together so I could wear it. Then she'd finish off the seams some other time.

The coat was a kind of plaid. It wasn't a large Scotch plaid, but it was a kind of a dull finish plaid. It had green and brown in it. It was real pretty. And of course it was beautiful material, real rich looking, you know. It wasn't cheap, you know. You could buy a lot of clothes that was cheap clothes, and then they looked like they're cheap when they're on you, but this one didn't. So that was that.

And then she had to go and find some buttons to suit that. And so she got some buttons and put them on. And then, she could send it somewhere else to get the buttonholes made if she didn't have time to do it. The buttons were great big, matched the green or the brown that was in the plaid.

Minnie Rose Lovgreen

So anyway, she took this job at Mrs. Cline's place, and she got along very well with it. And so this man, the chauffeur across the road from us, he said he would help, so. They all had trunks, you know. Everybody that come from the old country had trunks. So she said she had a big trunk to take, and she had to bring this trunk along, so Mr. Steele he came along, and he took one end of the trunk, and we took one end of it, and we walked along till we found this place, and then we moved in, moved her in there. And I still stayed with my job.

But this lady, they had prayers every morning That was another thing Celine didn't like. They had prayers every morning in the house. Soon as breakfast was over, they'd all go in the dining room, and kneel down by the chairs, and the man said the prayers. So Celine didn't like that, because she was a Catholic, see. She didn't like those prayers. She said would they mind if she didn't go in to prayers. And they said well, it was customary to have everybody go in to prayers. But she hadn't had prayers at the other place.

Well anyway, this Mr. Steele helped to carry this trunk up, and so she got all her things moved there. And I don't think hardly any of us had telephones those days, so we couldn't talk to each other very much. But if she got done she'd run quick over to where I lived to see how I was getting along, you know. And tell me how she was getting along. And so, that favorite word of hers, "Sacrustee," which means "Oh my goodness," you know, something different.

Well, she stayed there for quite a while. She was general, did everything. Cook and clean house and–well, you didn't do it as good as you do otherways. You have to plan the meals and so you're busy most of the time, but that was a general, general there, so she thought she'd get along. I don't think there was any children there. If they did, I didn't hear much about them.

So then she'd go down to see my parents every time I went down, and we went to parties and stuff like that. She began to talk more and more, better English and better English, and she wanted to sing. So, her and I we went to a place once, and they were having a little sing, and everybody had to do somepin' so we sang a duet, and that was "Down by the old mill stream/Where I first met you." And she just loved that song. She'd poke me along if I wasn't comin' along with the singin' you know.

She was pretty well educated in Belgium, and just a little bit older than I was. Just a little bit, a couple of years or so. I was pretty good at singing, but she'd perk me along and make me come up–she didn't want me to lag behind.

Then when we was ready to go from wherever we was setting at the table–if we was going to leave right after dinner or anything like that, or after tea–we'd touch each other with our foot under the table, and that was an indication that we both agreed that we're going to leave after the meal was over, and go somewhere else, go down and meet our boyfriends or somepin' like that, see. So we each had a boyfriend, so we went and met them and walked around the park.

She didn't go out with that Mr. Steele, that chauffeur. She wanted me to go out with him, but I didn't care for him anyway. He never explained himself. You couldn't get any sense out of him, you know. I mean you couldn't get any, you didn't know where he came from. He came from London, England, I knew that, but outside of that he never explained himself, so we never bothered with him. So we each had a boyfriend for a while

So by that time she had made me a new whipcord suit then. And it was cutaway style, where they had them cut around the corners, there, they didn't come down square. She said that suit looked good on me, and I wasn't too stuck on the cutaway style, because I liked everything to land square, but she said it looked real good on me.

And then she got to makin' hats. And she'd go to the ten-cent store and got this buckram hat (frame) made of white just like cheesecloth all starched, you know, and then take some blue silk and cover it, and she put daisies all the way around it and two little ribbons hangin' down the back. So I really felt stunning in that, yeah. Then I got some blue stockings and blue shoes to go with it. They was wearin' the dark stockings then, them days. That was still about 1912, you know.

Well, I told you when we went to meet all those people (relatives) down in there, to meet the train–and we went so many nights and the train hadn't come in, and then finally the train came in. They all had to go to different houses because there was so many of them. Wherever they had a relative or halfways a relative, some of them went there. And two of them went to my brother's place, and they each had a baby the same age. And they each had a comforter to suck on like they do now, you know, those little pacifiers, yes. They called them dummies those days. And each had a little dummy.

Far As I Can Remember

The babies were just about the same age and they both had these pacifiers. They laid the babies on a bed in the other room while they had tea and cake, you know. So I went in and looked at the babies. I couldn't figure out how they could lay those 2 babies down there close together. So when I came out I said, "Well, you sure will be in a mess now."

The mothers asked, "Why?"

And I said, "Well, you won't know which is which when you go to pick up your babies." And I really meant it. I know I wasn't very mature, that's for sure. But I looked older 'cause I wore all black clothes, you know, like dark clothes. I wasn't in for loud colors or anything like that. I didn't know anything about beauty or anything. Mine was just to keep going, gettin' ahead.

So anyway, when I said to these mothers, "You really won't know when you go to pick those babies up, which is yours—they both look alike," I really meant it, you know. And they looked at me and one of 'em said. "Wait till you get married. You'll know which is which."

And I've often thought of that ever since. What a dumb thing it was for me to say you wouldn't know which was which on their babies. You see them suckin' on those little dummies, those little pacifiers you know, and they both looked the same, and they were both boys, you know. And one was Frank and one was Benny.

Of course, I'd taken care of other children, but I wasn't really interested in them as much as I was driven to it. I'm interested in them now. I developed a liking for them. I can see the beauty of children now, but I didn't then.

Minnie Rose Lovgreen

I just knew I had to look after them, and you didn't have the only say. What the parents said, you had to do. You didn't have any other say over them, and that was that. If they wanted to kick you, they could kick you. If they wanted to take an apple, and take some bites out of it, and wouldn't give you any of it, well then, you just had to, just had to live with it, see. That was the way it was in them days.

So anyway, all these people then, the next day or so, they went to hunt jobs and go their various ways, you know, and they got work and they got goin' on things, and 'course they were real poor, you know–they'd sold up all their things to come over, and they'd used all their money.

But after they got goin'–they've got beautiful homes now and they're really wealthy–compared to what, you know. And they took a long time to get goin', but now their homes are beautiful and they take a big pride in 'em just like, you know– just like when you never had anything new before, and now you've got that new thing–you're sure gonna take good care of that. So they were all glad they came over.

Two of my cousins bought a bowling alley, and they had that for years, and years, and they made a very good success of it. They were very good business people. They all seemed to have business heads on 'em when they got goin', got away from the farm, you know.

Nobody went back to England to live. They went back on a visit. If they went back on a visit, they'd go all perked up, and come back again after they'd been over there, you know, and tellin' the people what a wonderful country this is, and makin' the other people feel they wanted to come over, too. So, little by little, some drifting ones come over.

But I had three sisters and a brother that was left in England, and they never came over. Because they were married—oh, three sisters—because they were married and they couldn't leave their husbands. And their husbands asked me if they could get a job if they come over, and I said, if you wasn't too choicy about the work you wanted to do, if you were willing to do anything that come your way, that was the thing. But if you were choicy about what you wanted to do, then you better not come, because you just couldn't pick and choose, see.

One of them had worked in Chivas Jam Factories for thirty-five years. You know, there's Chivas jams all over the world and Chivas marmalade, and his son has just graduated from there. He worked there for forty-five years. So you see, they get a job and they stick to 'em. They don't float around.

Anyway, all of these people who came to Canada, even some of the wives, went to work when they found out what good money they could earn just ironing for people. See, we didn't have drip-dry clothes then, so ironing had to be done, and laundry had to be done, so. And if it was laundry, they used to have to carry the big wash boiler up from the basement and cook them on the gas stove, you know. Cook the clothes, boil the clothes there, and then pack 'em all the way down.

So Celine did all that. She left that place, finally, the Clines' and she got another job in a doctor's family. And when they found how good she was at sewing, making things, they would take her off of the housework and off of the things, and bring some material in for her to make their dresses and hats and clothes that they wanted.

And they would be 'sposed to do her work while she was on this dressmaking job. But she said they did such a poor job that when she got through, she had an awful lot of cleaning to do. She was very particular about her cleaning, you know. I guess they were trained that way in Belgium. All the corners had to be gone into, and scrubbing had to be done.

So she was with this doctor's family for quite a while, and one day she dropped the iron on her toes. She was ironing and the iron fell off and dropped on her toes, and the doctor came in and asked her what she was fussing about, and she stood there holding one foot up and sayin' "Ouch, ouch," you know. And the doctor said, "What's the matter?"

And she said, "Well, I dropped the iron on my toes."

"Oh no," he said. "Celine is ironing her toes. You don't need to iron your toes out." You know, he teased her and she had to laugh then. He always said somepin' to make her laugh, you know, 'cause she'd forget about it. He thought that was the best thing to do. She stayed with them for quite a while, and then she'd come and see me wherever I was on her day off, you know, wherever I was working at.

Well, then she met Charlie (Clayton) and she got married to him. She didn't want to get married to him, but she did, finally. He talked her into it, and talked her into it, till he finally won. And he had a little boy. He'd been married before. He had little Arthur. His wife had died, so Celine was goin' to take care of little Arthur.

And the people next door to her that was his in-laws didn't like him marrying a Catholic, because she would bring up their child a Catholic, and they didn't want to see little Arthur brought up a Catholic. But anyway, she didn't have nothin' to do with his religion, so when Arthur got a little older he went to see the priest, and the priest talked him into it. So he became a Catholic anyway, no matter what. So that was that.

Charlie was interested in me for a long time. He said he was gonna have one of us girls 'cause he always saw us together. And I knew it wasn't gonna be me, so I always turned my head the other way. I knew it wasn't gonna be me. I could shunt 'em off when I wanted to. So he finally talked to her and talked to her, and he finally got her. It was a good thing because they had the wedding in their house, and I went there, helped them out with the wedding.

I made her wedding cake. I made a three-tier fruitcake. That was what they had for wedding cakes them days. And I got all these little silver balls and silver leaves and put on, you know, like they have, little peppermint things. Then I went down to town, and I banked the stove up and left this in the woodstove, mind you, this cake with a pan of water in there.

I went down to Vancouver, and bought the bride and bridegroom with the little bell and some forget-me-nots on. And I remember that cake just like it was yesterday. She was so happy with that cake. It was a great big cake. It was three tiers, you see, a heavy, solid fruitcake.

And so Charlie got a job. And then he was away out where he couldn't write to her. And she thought he just married her and dumped this little boy off onto her. And then she was stuck there with the house and almost nothing to eat, you know, and the neighbors next door wantin' to fight every time they saw her come home.

She went and stood in front of my brother's, walked up and down in front of my brother's house all day, until it was time for Charlie to come home after he come back from Swift Current. He finally come back after they harvested down there, or hayed, or somepin' like that. And he made a stake, then.

So then when he came back from there, they decided they'd have a fish and chip restaurant. So, just like that, they went and rented the place, and he knew how to clean the fish and how to get a Chinaman to do all the potatoes, the string potatoes. And she looked after the cash register that she was real good at, and he wasn't. And he looked after all the cooking and fish–fish cleaning, and everything like that. And they sold the fish and chips, a whole plateful, all a person could eat, for 15 cents a plate. And all the bread and butter you could eat with it, too. That was on Hastings, East. Hastings Street.

There were one or two other fish and chip places, but they weren't the old country like his was. His was the best. He was from Wales. And then they give 'em better, they give 'em a little better service, and a little bit better food probably.

And then that was during World War I. The war broke out, see, and all the soldiers would go in there and have fish and chips. So they did a raging business with all the soldiers goin' in there. Well, they couldn't serve any beer in there, but the soldiers could take a bottle of beer in with them, and nobody said anything about that, so they had that with their fish and chips.

But people didn't stay too long, you know. They come and eat their fish and chips and went out again. And Charlie, he looked after the counter. He got so he could look after the counter, in between acts of cooking. And she looked after all the tables.

And then when I had a day off, I'd go and help them. And I looked after the tables then when I was there. They paid me somethin', but then they didn't have to pay me much. 'Cause, you see, when I had a day off, I was living at their place, sleeping at their place, so I really didn't feel that they owed me anything, because I really owed them for lettin' me stay there.

You see, I had left that place where I was working, to go to a place where they had a small baby. And they had a nurse there, a Miss Weeks, a registered nurse. She wouldn't let them go in to see the baby. And they was afraid of her, so they didn't go in anyway. She kept saying no, you better not go in. And the baby died. And that was a terrible thing.

So after the baby died, of course, they had a lot of expense, what with the nurse and the doctors, and so on and so forth. I don't know what was the matter with the baby. I wasn't old enough, and interested, and she, the nurse, never hardly talked to me anyway, you know. She was uppity uppity, and so.

So anyway those people, then. I met an old astrologer man— a man that talked astrology. And he said, "Don't take too much stock on these people, because they're climbing up the ladder so fast they're goin' to come down in an awful hurry one of these days. He meant to say that they're goin' to go broke.

And so, they had bought some land on Shaughnessy Heights–that's in Vancouver, B.C.–and so they was goin' to build a house there. And it was the first house that was being built up there, so there was a lot of excavating to do with a big bulldozer. So while they were goin' to build this house, they said they wouldn't have enough money to finish the house, because the land cost so much. It was cheap then, but it isn't now. The land cost so much, and the house would cost so much to build, so that they didn't wanta' spend more than they had.

Well, he (the astrologer) said they would have to sit on apple boxes because they didn't have any furniture. See, the house they rented when they had the baby was furnished. And so then these two young people–they was about twenty-five and twenty-seven years old–they were both born in the same month–they were both Geminis. And the old astrologer said they were both of the same mind. They were goin' to come down with an awful crash, so he said, "You can't be sure of your job."

So the lady came in and said to me, you know, she said, "We haven't any money. Now you can stay here, for your meals, and help around a little bit, but if you get another job why it's all right to go to it. We like you, but we haven't got any more money to pay out."

So the milkman came and I told the milkman I was lookin' for another job, that these people were goin' broke. So he went down to Point Grey where they built the big university, and he told this lady down there, "If you ever want anyone to help you in the house," he said, "I know of an awful good girl. She's from England, and she's looking for a job, because the people went broke where she's working."

So she asked where it was and he told her. So she had a horse—they didn't have cars then. She had a horse, so she got on horseback and she came down to call on me.

She said, "Are you Miss Enefer?" and I said yes. So she said, "Well, I would like to hire you if you want a baby job, because we're goin' to have our first baby and you can help us a lot with that." So it was really wonderful that she came after me on horseback, see. She said, "Well, we'll arrange some way to get your trunk. I still had a trunk, you know. So she arranged somehow to get my trunk and they got me over to their place.

Celine wasn't married yet then. Later I made her cake at this house. They let me make the cake there. So that was my first babysitting job, really—the first one I liked. So they had the baby, a little boy, little John, and later I named my John after him 'cause he was such a cute little boy. And he grew up to be an awful fine little fellow.

Well, his father was an architect–he was a leading architect. He didn't look very important at all, but he was a lot more important than he looked like. And he won in the competition to build that university out at Point Grey. It's a beautiful university. It's been added to from time to time.

So he and his men studied for six days and six nights. He had twelve men and he won in the competition for building. He had the best architecture, the best picture, the best picture drawn of the university, what it should be and everything, you know. He was from Suffolk, England, and that's right on the border of Norfolk where we was born.

And I wasn't particular what I did. If a load of wood come, I'd get out there and stack it, you know. I'd just as soon be out there and stack the wood. And then she said she meant to have him kill a rabbit. They was goin' to have rabbit for dinner, and she couldn't get anybody to kill a rabbit. And of course, the war, you know. There wasn't too much meat or food around. So I said, "I can kill a rabbit."

She says, "You can kill a rabbit?"

I said, "Sure, I can kill a rabbit—'cause I done all those things—and skin it and everything else." So she went and got the rabbit, and I just hung him up by the tail and give him one big clip behind the ears, and he was gone. That was how we used to kill 'em at home. Just give 'em one great big clip behind the ears and he was gone. So we did the rabbit.

And then if the Hindu brought a great big load of wood when I was out there with the baby in the buggy, I'd stack the wood. And she was so amazed at me doing all these things. And I said that was because we were used to doing it. We were used to doing it. We didn't stack wood, but we stacked turf at home. And so, she was very happy about that. I couldn't see that wood all laying around there like that.

So then they stopped all the building of the University, because the war got so bad, and they took her husband to draft men to go overseas, because he was a captain in the African war. He was Captain Sharp then, see, and so they knew that he had a lot of experience, so they took him to train men to go overseas. So every time he trained a big battalion to go overseas, he'd come and ask me to make them a great big cake.

Quantity rather than quality, that was. You'd cook the raisins and everything, you know, and then stir everything in with it, and apples, and stir 'em all in with it, you know, and then cook it, and it was like a great big fruit cake. But he always give 'em coffee and cake as a send-off after they got all trained.

So he trained one battalion after another. First of all, they picked out all the biggest and the handsomest men, and then, when they were gone, they picked out the second size, and the third size, until they got down to the bantam regiment. And they were all small men. The big men was all gone first, see.

They had the Scotch Kilties, too. He trained the Kilties, too. The Kilties, you know, had the bagpipes. So he trained them. So then they told him that he couldn't go ahead with the University. All buildings had to be stopped. And all operations of everything had to be stopped that didn't concern the war. Everybody's mind should be turned toward winning the war.

So I thought well, if that's the case then, I might as well quit my job and go and make ammunition. So I figured, well, that lady could look after her own baby, and I might as well go and make ammunition in the ammunition factory, 'cause she wasn't goin' to make it. Well, she didn't mind. She told me to come back after the war ended.

So I used to go back and see her real often. We were friends, and her little John was just getting to where he was pulling himself up by chairs—I guess about nine or ten months old. He was a cute little boy. He was awfully good.

Then, of course, her husband had to go to war then. After he'd trained all the men, there was nothing left for him to do but to go to war himself. So they took him in then, and he was up in the aeroplane takin' pictures of what was goin' on down below. So that was his job then, see. He wasn't flyin' the plane, but he was takin' the pictures so they could show how the war was goin' on, you know. 'Course everybody read the casualties list every night.

So I was there making ammunition until the war ended, and then, when the war was ended, I went back again and worked for them. The war ended in 1918. November the 11th, 1918. World War I.

Chapter Four

1917-1920

Marriage~Motherhood~Changes

~ "I married this fellow we didn't like."

~ "They had to go and flag the train."

~ "…and away we went on the ferry."

So then I stayed there a while, and then I got married from there. I married this fellow that we didn't like, this chauffeur down there that we met down the West End. He was the one I married. His name was Jack Steele.

Well, Celine was telling me that there wouldn't be any good men coming back from the war, that they would all be killed off, and if I was waiting for some special person, they wouldn't be comin' back, so I would be lucky if I got him. I would be so lucky if I got him, I could just kiss my hands if I got him. I couldn't see it, but I thought, well, I've always done more or less what she asked me to do, so I guess I'll marry him and see how it goes. Oh no. It was a rotten deal, the whole thing through.

Minnie Rose Lovgreen

There was one man that I liked very much, and he said for me not to wait, because he said I was young then.

And he said, "If you get a chance to marry someone else, I would suggest that you marry, because we don't know whether we'll come back or not." He said, "You never know in war. Everything's fair." So. He was a real nice man. He was Scotch.

So anyway, we got married , and then he said, "Well now we have to go home and look after the greenhouses." He had two greenhouses, you know. So we went right out where he had greenhouses, to his house, you know.

So anyway, when we got over there to his house there, he showed me the greenhouses and all the cucumbers and everything comin' up, and told me which benches I had to water in the morning. We would grow tomatoes and cucumbers and gladiolas. And the cucumbers were grown, so they climbed up. They were tied to wires, so they were off the ground. Then there was a bed at the bottom, and in this bed was peat moss and all good soil that would make growth. Then we put lettuce in there.

I knew some about greenhouses when we were married– but not too much–because this lady (Mrs. Shelton) where I first worked when I left home, she had a little greenhouse of her own, and I used to give her a hand once in a while.

Anyway, I had to go in the greenhouses by six o'clock in the morning in the summertime, start watering, and start cleaning off and picking off the dead leaves and so on, and stirring up the soil on the south bench, and on the east bench. And of course I fell for all that.

He said it was no use to feel that I had to monkey around in the house, because there wasn't any bread and butter in that. We had to stick to the greenhouse work. So he'd go somewhere, and deliver big cans of milk somewhere that he'd picked up alongside the road. Take them in to a dairy. That was his job. He never came home till twelve o'clock at night, no time. And so I was there all day, and way till twelve o'clock at night.

And it was a miserable little house. Two rooms. I think there was a living room and a kitchen all in one, and then a bedroom and that's all there was to it. The rain was coming in the top. You had to hang a bucket up to catch the rain. It was really a miserable affair, you know. I knew I was in for it, and I said to my stepmother, I said, "Well, if I don't like this, I guess I can get away from it."

"Well," she said, "watch out you don't get pregnant so you can't get away from it." I remember her saying that—watch you don't get pregnant so you can't get away from it—but people didn't know anything about pills those days or anything like that, or taking anything so as not to get pregnant.

Marrying him was the biggest mistake I ever made, really. Exceptin' there's one thing I'm grateful for. I've got John. And I wouldn'ta had John if it hadn't been for that, see.

And when the men came—one night two men came, and they came and they wanted to see him, and I told them he wasn't in. They said what time would he be in, and I said well, lots of times he didn't get in till twelve o'clock, and they said well, they'd still sit and wait for him. So I didn't know anything about it.

So anyway, these men waited there till he came in, and then they told him that they were the sheriff and the bailiff, and they said he hadn't paid any rent for that place for three years. So I had to hear all that because there was no place for me to go. I had to set there and hear it all, so there wasn't a thing I could say, because he was the head of the house, you see–the man was the head of the house and you couldn't say anything.

So anyway, we had pigs and chickens and there was an old lame horse there. I think it was just grazing around there, and he said he owned it–somebody must have given it to him. It wasn't worth anything 'cause it was lame all the time and it was real old.

So he said, well, that old horse was an old friend of the family. He told the bailiff and the sheriff it was an old friend of the family. He didn't see that he could hardly part with that, and so finally he mussed around till he got quite a bit of money out of the horse anyway, no matter what, see.

So then he said, "The chickens belong to the wife (meaning me) She wouldn't even eat her breakfast till she'd gone out and fed them chickens in the morning. And the pigs belong to her." So that way they had nothing to play with. It all belonged to me, see. He would never tell me nothing.

He never told me nothing, see. I often asked about his parents, but he never would say nothing about them. So anyway, when he didn't get along up there, where he was goin' to grow these tomatoes, the men settled for all what was there on the farm, and of course we had to get out.

I said, "What are we goin' to do now?"

A 1917 Willis Knight touring car

And I said, "We're expecting our baby."

And so he said, "Well, we'll just have to go and live with some people in Vancouver that I know of. They'll take us in. They're junk dealers, but they'll take us in." I thought junk dealers sounded perfectly terrible, but junk dealers have money. They have money because they get junk and stuff from all over and sell it, and so and so forth. So anyway, we went through that. So there, we went to live with this junk dealer and his wife. His wife was very nice. And so she looked after me when I was pregnant.

So I didn't know what he was goin' to do next. I never knew what move he was goin' to make next. But before he left Vancouver, this was the funny part of it, he had a big Willis Knight, big old car called a Willis Knight that he used to haul the milk in. He could take the back seat out or somepin' like that, and put the cans in there, and it was a big, heavy, sturdy old car, about one of the strongest things that's made, I guess.

So he said, "I've sold that Willis Knight," and he said, "I want you to go tomorrow morning down to the bank, and soon." He said, "I sold it to a policeman, and I want you to go down to the bank, and soon's the bank opens I want you to cash that check he gave me right away." That was when I was in Vancouver, see. And it was just about two days before I had John.

So I went down to the bank. My husband said, "Be right there when the door opens, so you can go in, first one to go in." So I was right down at the bank, and they took the check in, and they said the policeman had already cancelled the check, 'cause my husband was a crook, you see. He was crooked. He never told me that he hadn't paid all that rent, and he didn't tell me nothing. So here I was. So I went and stayed there (at the junk dealer's) till the baby was born.

And so the baby was born right there in the house where we stayed. A doctor came, the same doctor that Celine worked for. He came and took care of the baby for thirty-five dollars, and the baby was tongue-tied, so he had to snip the tongue, 'cause he could only squeak like a little pig. Maybe the pig marked him, I don't know, when I was chasin' pigs, for goodness sakes. You never can tell, anyway. Then, when the baby was born, we went up to Kamloops, to a place called Val de Chine.

But I was happy with the baby. Oh, I was happy with the baby. I traveled with him a whole day's journey when he was

Minnie Rose and her son John

seven days old. And I was tired, too, I was really all in. So anyway, we stayed up at Val de Chine.

And he was goin' to grow tomatoes and cucumbers–tomatoes on the fields there because there was so much hot sun there. We were goin' to pick 'em and sell 'em in those little square boxes. Punnets they called them. They called 'em punnets, them little square boxes. They'd hold about, oh probably about, four or five pounds. It wasn't the smallest ones like the strawberry boxes—the other ones. Well anyhow, he

121

was goin' to do all that, but when he got there the ground wasn't all right, so he couldn't do it.

All of a sudden he decided that he would go to work on the railroad tracks. The only conclusion I could ever come to was that he was afraid of bein' conscripted, he didn't want to go into the war. And so he'd take all those jobs, anything at all, in order to keep out of the war. He was a local florist, that was his profession. He knew how to grow gladiolas and all those things in the greenhouses, you know, and have a big supply of them, everything comin' good. But he didn't stick to it. He'd plan all the work and then turn the job over to me, and then go and do some other thing. He never knew what he was doing. And I never got no thanks from him. If I had a dime in my pocket he'd find it, he wanted that, he'd have to have it, so.

So anyway, this is one thing I did when the hens weren't laying good. There was lots and lots of onions, gunnysacks full of onions, so I thought well, I've got to make those hens lay somehow, and it was wintertime and they didn't want to lay, and it was a wet miserable place they had. So I chopped up the onions real fine, chopped 'em up with one of those food choppers, you know, and mixed them in with the food, with the cooked food, and the chickens began to lay like everything. They wouldn't eat the onions to begin with, but they got starved down so they'd eat 'em anyway later on. So Jack wouldn't eat all the eggs. I didn't hardly eat eggs, but he did. He'd want all the eggs, probably have two or three, if they was there, you know, and if there wasn't any there, well then he couldn't have them.

I took the eggs and I hid 'em up in an old stove that stood outside. I let him have some for his breakfast, but the others I hid. And then when I had time I took 'em down to this doctor's family and sold 'em for a dollar a dozen. So I began to get some pocket money. So that was the only way I could get anything. I thought well, if he's goin' to be crooked with me.

So I put some eggs in an old box that stood there, and it had had Lifebuoy soap in it, and I never knew anything about that, so one day I tasted an egg and it tasted like Lysol. And I couldn't figure out what in the world had made that, what had the chickens eaten? It certainly wasn't onions. Whatever had they eaten to make their eggs taste like Lysol? So when I come to smell in that box, that box had had Lysol soap in it, that's Lifebuoy, and it tainted the eggs. Nobody ever complained, but believe me I knew enough not to put them in that tainted box any more. I learned that much.

Well, then we moved up to a place called Copper Creek. And we had a big house there. And it was clean, nothing in it. It was all wood, sort of a straight wood, where you'd scrub it down with a scrubbin' brush and soap and water. And there wasn't no linoleum or anything like that on the floors. There was a bed and a few chairs and a table. So he said, well, when we got up there I would have to board five men. I looked at the stove and it didn't look very good.

We went on the beach and picked our wood off the beach, and he picked some and I picked some, and we finally found out we could make bread, 'cause we had to make bread for the whole bunch of them, see. There wasn't no bakery there or no store or anything, and see, when they wanted meat, they had to go and shoot a groundhog or a woodchuck out there. So then they'd skin that and lay it in soda and water, bakin' soda, you know, and take out the animal flavor, and then we'd fry that and give 'em that.

And so the men all had to eat at our place, but they couldn't sleep there because there was no place to sleep, and they all had bunks alongside the road. So a dollar a day for all their meals. Each man paid a dollar a day and that fed them. We couldn't get meat, only once a week when we went up to Kamloops, and that was on payday.

Well anyway, there was no way of washing clothes. You had to take 'em down on the beach and wash 'em in the beach water, and put rocks on their corners to keep the diapers from flying away. Nobody ever put me up a clothesline. Nobody ever did anything to help with the house for me, to make anything easy.

So the stove got so it wouldn't cook, and I had to go to an old camp there, and I got a lot of those square cocoa tins. I fitted them all around, between the top of the stove and the oven, and ashes between them, and then the old thing cooked! I don't know how I ever thought of it, but it just seems like the things came into my head to do and I did 'em.

Anyway, one day I began to get fed up, and I thought, well this is the end of this. I can't see any future in this for me a'tall, and no future for John. So I said to him one morning–he'd gotten up kind of angry–and I said to him, "Now listen. Well, I'm gettin' tired of you gettin' up angry every morning for no reason a'tall. If you don't like your job you shouldn't have taken it, you should have taken somethin' else."

And he said he didn't want any of my back talk or anything like that, and I said, "Well, I'll tell you one thing now. I'm goin' to give you two weeks to straighten out and act like a man, and if you can't act like a man and a husband and a father to this child, then," I said, "I'm goin' to go back down to Vancouver." We was a day's journey from Vancouver.

And he said, "Well, you can't go, you can't take the child with you."

And I said, "Yes, I can. You can't take a nursing baby away from its mother." And I was still nursing him, you see, and I did it on purpose. I said, "You can't take a nursing baby away from his mother." John was about fifteen months old. He was beginning to walk around, you know.

So I give him two weeks to straighten out. And he didn't give me any money. He collected the money from the men, soon's the men paid their board money. He collected all that, and I never knew what he did with it all, but we never saw any money, there wasn't any money a'tall.

So I had a few chickens up there, and then we had two or three pigs up there, too. So one morning we was chasin' the pigs in and they got out, and I was helpin' to chase them in so we wouldn't lose them. So his boss came along and he saw me tryin' to get the pigs in, so he came along and helped to get the pigs in. So then my husband came along then, and he was mad then, because the boss was helpin' me get the pigs in. He acted like he was jealous. He wouldn't talk to nobody.

So the boss said, "What's the matter with that guy?"

I said, "I don't know. I don't have the slightest idea."

"Is he jealous?"

"I don't know. Maybe he is."

"Well, why don't you give him somepin' to be jealous for?"

"No. I haven't given him anything to be jealous for, and I don't intend to. I'll tell you one thing. He's got one more week now. He's had two weeks to straighten out, and if he doesn't straighten out by the first of the month, then I'm goin' to Vancouver. And I'm not goin' to ever come back, so you'll have to find another place to let your men board."

And that house was immaculately clean. It was scrubbed, and smelled clean, and everything. But every night the bedbugs fell down from the ceiling, and came and got around our necks, and in our beds, and everywhere, and around John's neck, and I had to get up and take him away in the nighttime.

And so we finally moved our bed outside, right out in the open, and put a canvas over it from one knob to the other. They had a head and a foot to it, and then we crawled under that, and then we could sleep without being eaten up by the bedbugs. And John's buggy was out there and he slept in his baby carriage. He never had a bed, never did have a bed. He slept in the corner on the floor, when he wasn't sleeping in the buggy. When he got older he slept in the corner on the floor.

I had to move around. I never could take care of beds and buggies and stuff like that, so everywhere I went, if I bought a new buggy or a pushcart or a little stroller or anything like that, I'd have to leave it there, and go on to the next place, and hope to pick up another one like it just as cheap as I could haul that around. So when he saw us goin' to Vancouver, he said, "You can't take all the wedding presents."

And I said, "Well, the wedding presents–what there are that my folks gave me–I'll take, and the ones that your folks give you, well, you can keep." 'Course they didn't. They hadn't given him any.

"Oh, is that so?" I was much sharper than he thought I was, 'cause they say a worm will turn around once in a while when he gets goin.'

So when it come the train time, they had to go and flag the train, so his boss was nailin' down the box of china, my china, and my sewin' machine. He was nailin' down the box of china and that.

So he came along and he said, "I'll nail that down for her, I'll nail that down."

And the boss said, "No. I started and I'm goin' to finish it."

So he didn't have enough to say to him. He was a big Eyetalian guy and he better be stayin' away from him. So anyway, we got them nailed down and we carried the baby up to the train depot, and we got on the train, and thank goodness to bad rubbish.

I was so glad to get out of there. I never even give it one more thought about goin' back or anything of the kind. He got in jail–he'd done somepin' and then he got in jail up there. Takin' somepin' that didn't belong to him or somepin' like that, and so he got in jail.

And so his jail warden's wife wrote to me and she said, "How could you be so mean as to take the child away where his father couldn't see him?" And I wrote and told her that she was welcome to him, she could have him. If she could see any good in him anymore. I couldn't see any help for me in that.

Then they asked me to come up and bring the baby up for some reason or other. I don't know why. The same people that was the junk dealers moved up there. So they asked me to come up and stay with them for a couple of days, and they give my husband leave to come over and see the baby, to see how the baby was comin' along. And I had to go to the jail for some reason or other. I can't remember what that was for, but I had to go there. And the sheriff said, "Has he ever bought the child any shoes or socks or anything like that?"

"No, he's never bought him nothing. All the clothes has been given to him."

So he said, "For goodness sake, give that child some money to buy some shoes. You don't need that money." So he finally dug out two and a half dollars, I think, for some shoes for John. Shoes was pretty cheap. So then I went further up the road there. I went to Bury, then. Instead of goin' back to Vancouver, I went up to Bury. And got a job in a hotel cookin' then. So I cooked there for twenty-seven people.

I had John there with me for a little while, but I found out that I couldn't keep him there. There wasn't any comfort for him. I had to be in the kitchen by five in the morning–it was winter–and stay there till eight at night, and cook all the bread. And the water had to be hauled in and heated on the stove to wash dishes. There was three sitting downs at the table. They had three different meals to serve, and I had to cook the meals and serve the meals.

John was about eighteen to twenty months old. He was gettin' around. Oh, some of the people bought him a red knitted suit with gaiters on that come way under his feet. And then it went way up around his neck. And they was separate, so that the sweater was separate, and it came up high around his neck. And I bought him a little red hat to go with it and red mittens.

Some of the people up around there was sorry for him. They didn't like old Nelson, you know, that owned the hotel, see, so they were sorry for me bein' over there, so they wanted to get me away from there.

So the girl that was there before, I think, was ready to come back. And I told them that I was goin' to leave anyway, and so they said that I'd had some long distance calls. I couldn't get a long-distance call without I went in the other room where they all were. I'd only had one long-distance call, but he wanted me to pay so much on another one that I never had had. So I told him I wasn't goin' to pay for anything I never had had, see. So that was that. And his wife was diabetic, see. She was havin' to have special food. So that was the end of that story up there.

I don't know how I did it. Jobs were hard to get. People were short of money and everything, you know. So after a certain time, the people in the little grocery store sent a note over to say that if I didn't like my job not to stay there and work for them slave drivers– that I could go and stay up in their attic room there till the train come, if I wanted to go back to Vancouver. So somebody must have told them.

They didn't want to see the little boy suffer, so they left me a thermos and some sandwiches there in this attic room, and when the time came for me to go to the train, one of the men that I was feeding at the hotel there, that used to sit at the table, came over and carried the baby up to the train. We had to walk through snow up to our waist. I don't know how we did it. One o'clock in the night we flagged the train. That was the time the train went through.

I never got to see the men exceptin' they come in the kitchen. They weren't really allowed in the kitchen, but they saw me when I was at the table. There was a Mr. Roryson. I think he was a Norwegian fellow. He was the one that carried the baby up to the train, and then I had to carry the suitcases, and whatever else we had. I didn't have too much anyway. The diapers and stuff like that. I guess I was a ragamuffin.

Then I went back to Vancouver, and I went back to work for those same people I worked for before, that came and got me on horseback. And they were glad that I'd come. So I found out that John and their John was not too very well, because their John was only one by himself and my John was only one by himself. We decided that I'd find another place to board John, so I boarded John out then. There they had three other little boys.

By that time Celine and Charlie had moved to Seattle. And so they wrote to me and asked me if I wouldn't like to come and see Seattle, and see if I'd like it out there. So I thought, well, that's a good opportunity. I think I'll do that. I packed up my things and I packed up John's things and away we went on the boat.

Chapter Five

1920-1955

Seattle~Bainbridge Island~Marriage~Dairy

~ *"There was so much freedom here. I felt free."*

~ *"We both took hard jobs."*

~ *"We lived in a house with a lot of flowers."*

~ *"It was really a wonderful life."*

When I got to Seattle, the Claytons took me in and they were real nice. And then I liked it so much that I thought I'd like to get a job and work here–there was so much freedom here. I felt free. I felt like I wasn't pinned down or something like that. So Celine said, "Well, you'll have to go to the immigration office."

So we went to the immigration office the next day, and the immigration office man said, "Well, you can pay a head tax right here, and then you can stay, if you're sounded out by the doctors. So John and I got sounded out by the doctors, and then we got to stay. So we never did go back.

I got divorced then. I went with Mr. Ramsborg. I heard he was real good. He was an old German attorney and he was real good and he got me a divorce. I think I only had to pay fifty dollars. But nobody come to comply against me, or anything like that.

So I stayed in Seattle then. I found a place to put John to board with a German lady. She was an awfully nice old "mutter" we called her. And so we let him stay there,

And she had children that could take care of John, and lead him out in the afternoon when they came home from school, and stuff like that. And he was just in his glory to be there. They were real nice to him. I only earned thirty-five dollars a month and I had to give them twenty-five dollars. And then later on they wanted thirty dollars, so I only had five dollars for myself then.

But Celine still made my clothes, so you see that was a help to me. Or if I bought something, she'd go downtown and she'd say, "Oh you really must have a different suit than that, you've had that so long." So then finally she would say, "Well, that would be all right. I could give a little alteration on that," so she would alterate it.

I looked around to find a place to board John. Finally I found a German lady, Mrs. Schukar. She decided to take care of him for me. She had some children that was going to high school, so they could help out. She lived near Cowan Park. He boarded there and they were very good to him, so I could get me a job then, general—that was cooking and doing housework and everything, you know.

So I did that for a while, and finally I decided that I would take up baby nursing again, that I liked it better. So I got with a Mrs. Paul Smither, and she was coming to Bainbridge Island for a summer vacation, to rent a house for the summer. So I came with her and I took care of the children over here.

And then later on, I left her and I went to work for Mrs. Leo Black on Bainbridge Island. They had a baby, and I took care of that baby then, until the time I got married again. That was Marilyn Black. She was one month old when I went there, so I took care of her for over a year.

So on Bainbridge Island, I went down to visit the dairy farm, there was a dairy farm there. And I'd always wanted to be either a dairyman's wife, or a breadman's wife, or something that meant something, that they had to produce.

So I thought I'd go and see this dairyman who was working with the farm there. And he liked me right away, and I kind of liked him, but I wasn't quite sure. He was Danish. He looked real healthy and well. I went to see the dairy farm, and of course he was milking the cows there. I didn't know anything about him then.

And then the people at the Country Club gave parties, and they wanted us to go to the parties. We went to all the parties then. He could dance quite well, and so I danced, too, we danced at the parties, and he was very good.

We danced the Swedish polka and the schottische. And some waltzes. And then we had a medley waltz. That's where they all join hands and go round, you know. I liked music and dancing, and of course he did too, very much. I had a pretty little yellow dress with black spots on it, and I liked that very much.

Leo wasn't much taller than me and people wondered where that little couple came from all of a sudden. Leo was short, a real round face with rosy cheeks. And he was always happy. He smoked a pipe. So everybody was trying to do something for us, to make us happy. So anyway, in a year or so we got married.

We went to Oregon when we was married, for our honeymoon. When we came back, 'course he had to come back to do some more work in that dairy. We both took hard jobs when we thought we could make a go of it. It was after that that I took up this baby route work.

I had a baby route at the Country Club. I used to go and pick up the babies and bathe them and make their formula for the day, and then go on to the next house and do the same there. It took me till about eleven o'clock to get all the babies done, a little bit over an hour at each place. And then I'd go home and get my husband's lunch and my lunch, and little John was with us then– we'd got him back–so he got his lunch.

Then I would have a rest, and then I would go right back and start picking up the babies again and give them their lunches. There were about six babies. They were in all different houses.

By that time I was expecting Junior, and the people that had those other babies couldn't go in the bathroom because they were pregnant and they had morning sickness, but I could go in the bathroom. It didn't bother me one little bit, so no one knew that I was expecting.

But we didn't have modern conveniences, so we had to set the children on an ironing board to bathe them and to change their diapers and everything like that. We didn't have these proper little bassinets like people have nowadays. It was sort of a makeshift place.

Anyhow then this went on. I picked the babies up till about three o'clock and then took some of them to the beach for a little walk, a little stroll. And then I would go home. Someone else would put them to bed. They didn't have to have a bath at night.

Then I would go out for the evening and wait table wherever they was having a dinner party. If I didn't wait table, I cooked the dinner. So it just depended. Wherever there was a dinner party, they'd call me. And sometimes it was in the same house. Sometimes the work lasted till one o'clock in the morning. And we didn't have any lights, any electricity.

My husband had been working at that dairy for eleven years, so he was milking the cows, and cleaning out the barn, and delivering some of the milk and meeting the ferry boats (part of the Mosquito Fleet, the privately operated marine transportation systems on Puget Sound) that came in at the Country Club, to take passengers where they wanted to go, and work like that.

But he had to get up at one o'clock in the morning to go out and get the cows, so he didn't have too much time. After that he went home and rested. So when he went home to get his sleep, he always took the newspaper with him, and he'd have his breakfast, and he'd go right down, right in his room with the newspaper, and fall asleep right away, and sleep until almost one o'clock again. Then he'd get up and have his lunch, and start getting the cows in again. And that was every day the same thing.

Minnie Rose Lovgreen

He'd left Denmark when he was thirteen years old, so he was mostly going to school in Denmark. He got on one of the ships as a stoker, you know, building the fires, keeping the fire going. And then somehow or other, later on, he got to this country that way.

And then he worked in a dairy at Mt. Vernon, Washington, for a while, and he worked in a dairy in Alaska. That was before I met him. And the dairy in Alaska was the Kramer Dairy. It's right near Anchorage. And when he came from Alaska, he worked near Bellingham in a dairy up there for a while.

And then World War I broke out in 1914, and he went into World War I, and he was there till almost the end of the war. He was in the Army, all over different parts of England. He didn't go back to Denmark. He never did go back to his home after he left it. Thirteen years old. He never did go back to see them or anything until close to the end of his life.

There were seven children in his family. His father had left when he was a little boy, and the mother raised the seven children by herself. The father run off with someone else. I think he went to Argentina. I don't know what he had in Argentina, but it seems like they had money and he went to Argentina.

After the war he worked around Mr. Vernon for a while, and then he worked at the Carnation Dairy. That was it. He was at the Carnation Dairy in what they called the "test barn." They had to milk every four hours, so he would go to sleep, and when his four hours sleep was up, he'd have to get up and start milking again. But they wanted to see how much milk they could get from the cows by milking them every four hours.

So they had this large cow called Petra Segis, a large Holstein cow that was giving a lot of milk. And her udder was so big that you had to put like a dishpan under her to get the milk, it was so close to the ground. Then you had to milk her from two sides. So that was a tough job, but he took that. He took the tough jobs anyway.

It was after that he came to the Country Club. He saw an ad in the paper where he could work at that dairy there, so he'd been there eleven years when I met him.

We lived in a house with a lot of flowers. There was about 6 steps up, and on each step he had a little tub of flowers, and they were very pretty. They were geraniums and sweet alyssum, and they lit that whole little place up.

Minnie Rose on the beach

And they thought he was the real gardener. There was a gardener living next door to us, but the gardener next door to us didn't have any flowers. They didn't think that was the gardener's place, so they came to our place to see the gardener, and my husband said he wasn't the gardener, he was the dairyman. Well, they said, your place looked like you would be the gardener with all the things you have. We had snapdragons, too, and ivy geraniums that crawl down, that creep down the box, you know, and look pretty. They were pink and some red, too.

It was a wooden house, but we had someone build us a fireplace, so we could get the bark off the beach and use the bark for the fireplace. It was very good for the fireplace. There was one large living room, one bedroom at that time, and we added on another bedroom.

We didn't own the place—we just rented it at that time for five dollars a month because we worked at the dairy. And then we got one or two quarts of milk a day for our family, an allowance for working at the dairy. And my husband's wages was only eighty-five dollars a month then. So I had to get out and help.

It was really a wonderful life, being right by the water. And John was old enough so he'd go down and throw up the bark off of the beach onto the bank, and then when it dried he'd wheel it in, you know. He was about five years old then, so he was getting along. He could do things with his little wagon.

Then we had a few chickens. We always had chickens. We didn't have any ducks there. Just had the chickens. And we sold eggs, and people would like our eggs very much, so when

John got a little older he would deliver the eggs on the bicycle. So that was quite a help. He delivered a lot of eggs on the bicycle.

My husband took a big interest in John and took him out wherever he went. He always took him along with him. We didn't have a car then. Later on we bought a car, and it was an old Ford, so we had to wind it up to make it go, you know the ones you had to wind them up to make them go.

So anyway, when I went to work in the evening, waiting table or cooking or something, they told me not to get in trouble with the cook. If the cook thought she knew it all, just let her think she did know it all, and if I could help her then that would be all right, but if I did help her, then I pretended not to know anything about it, so I would do it the way she wanted me to. That way I got along with the cook.

But sometimes I wasn't coming home till one o'clock in the morning, and I had to have a candle in a coffee can for a flashlight, and I held that ahead of me so that I could find the way home, could see the pathway home. It was sometimes a mile to walk after you got through with work. No one brought you home or took you there. I don't think hardly anybody had that many cars to spare.

John took care of himself quite a bit. And then during the daytime–my husband was home during the day, you see, he'd be with John then. And then when I got home I would be with John, so that was that. He knew how to look after himself. There wasn't very many boys around there for him to play with. The caretaker there had a little boy named Edgar, and he used to play with John.

Then one day my ex-husband came, and he saw John, and John remembers him. That was when John did see him. John was coming on the school bus, and he said to him, "Do you know where Mrs. Lovgreen lives?" He'd gotten hold of my name somehow or other.

And John says, "Yes. She lives right down there at my house. I'll show you." So they were all on the school bus and John got off the school bus, and he said, "Well, my mother isn't home. She's working for somebody out in the Country Club today, but I can go out and get her."

He ran up to get me and he said, "Come on, quick. There's two nice gentlemen there and they want to talk to you. They have to see you right away." So I left what I was doing. We had a big garden tea that day, and when we had a big garden tea I was the chief waitress, you know, and of course I always had to be dressed real nice—no shoes running down at the heel—and a nice white apron and black dress with white cuffs and collar and stuff like that.

So I went down then to see what they wanted, and to my surprise it was him. I kind of thought it would be him. I don't know why. I didn't know who else could be coming to see me. And by that time John was seven years old, so you see, that's quite a long time after.

But he'd met somebody else in Victoria and he wanted to get married again. So he could get married in Victoria, he had to serve the papers on me first. He said if I went to Vancouver I still wasn't divorced, that I was only divorced over here, but I wasn't divorced in Vancouver. That wasn't true, though.

140

So he served the papers on me and he saw my husband, and he saw Junior, a little boy then, and he said, "He's a cute little boy, isn't he?"

So I just said yes and no and snapped him off and let him go. He had–not a bailiff–but an attorney with him that he got—DeCour, I think his name was. He was in Vancouver. He was one of the top lawyers there. So he'd have to pay him quite a bit.

So then when he went to marry this girl in Victoria, they were signing some papers about the place and about her place. She had a greenhouse thing, you know. I don't know what part of Victoria it was, but she had a greenhouse. So he wanted his name in on that, and they said, no, that belonged to the wife. So he didn't get in on that, he didn't horn in on that.

So anyway, he had a heart attack later and died. He always looked well. He always looked the same. He was short and stocky, good color and stuff like that. I never regretted leaving him. I just had that experience. Maybe it was a good thing I did.

When Junior was born we just had a doctor come to the house. And my sister-in-law from Vancouver, B.C., was staying with me at the time. He was a very strong baby. He was born about one o'clock in the morning and we didn't have any trouble with him a'tall. He was real good.

Both the boys were good and strong. They never had doctors. We never went to doctors with them after they were born. John was tongue tied a little bit when he was born, but the doctor fixed that tongue. John could only squeak, he couldn't cry. Like he couldn't lift his tongue up. It was tied down.

Well then, after the eleven years was up, they (The Country Club) decided that they wouldn't have a dairy there anymore. They wanted it all to be golf course. So they didn't have the dairy there anymore. Well then, when they closed the dairy there, we decided that we would have our own dairy because my husband couldn't find a job.

He went to Seattle every day to the employment office and he couldn't find a job, and he thought he'd go back to the Carnation Dairy. He wanted me to move up there, but I didn't want to move up there because I would lose my Country Club jobs, and with the babies, see, so I didn't think I would move up there. I could take John with me where I went to get the babies. They all liked him anyway. He was a cute little boy.

So anyway, my husband stayed at the Carnation Dairy for about a month, and then he wanted to know if I would go up, and I said no. I said we could rent a dairy here (on Bainbridge Island) and start working with our own dairy. By that time we had the other little boy, we had Junior then. And I said they'd soon grow up where they could start helping, and then I said it was better that way, so.

Then we decided to have our own dairy farm. So I said to my husband, let's go over and look at that dairy that Mr. Gill left. Gill had discontinued his dairy, and went over to Port Orchard to go in with another man over there. He didn't think he liked the Island any more. He thought the Island people much too snoopy, that they were all snoopin' into his business.

And he went broke in Port Orchard. They had to sell the

milk at five cents a quart. So he went broke. And so then he got a route where he would take fish to Chicago, I think it was, or someplace, and bring eggs back.

Well anyway, we decided to take the dairy that he didn't want any more on the Island. And it was a mess. There was tin cans and eggshells and stuff all over. We thought we'd clean that all up, so we went over and rented the dairy, or thought we did.

And when we came back my husband said, "I don't think I want that place after all." He changed his mind. He didn't think he wanted it. He'd go in town the next day and look for another job. He hadn't paid any deposit on the place, so he went to Seattle to look for another job. And he still come back shakin' his head. He didn't find another job.

So I said, "Well, I'll tell you. I'm going back to rent the dairy that you said you didn't want."

And he said, "Who's going to run it?"

I said, "Well, we'll come. We'll all come. We'll run it together. We'll all get goin' on it." So we went over, and we told the old gentleman that we wanted to rent his dairy.

He said, "You were here yesterday and you changed your minds. I don't think you've got enough backbone."

And I said, "Well, I'm renting it this time."

"You're renting it?

I said, "Yes, I'm renting it and here's the deposit." He said he wanted a deposit down, so we paid him five dollars deposit down. So we went over and started to clean up the place, and I said, "We'll have to get some cows now. We're paying rent, so we'll get some cows and get started."

143

And my husband said, "Well, I can't find any cows." So he went to see someone in Seattle and look around some of the old dealers that we used to know at the Country Club, that used to come over there and bring us cows. And he didn't find any there. He said he couldn't find any cows.

So he told me, "You are so smart, you just find some cows."

So I thought, well, all right, I don't have to go to Seattle to find cows. I got goin' on the phone, and I phoned one of the dealers, and they said yes, they had cows, they'd bring us over six cows if we wanted six cows, and they'd all be milking. He said, "I'll bring you over 6 cows and a bull."

And I said, "Yes, we'll need a bull. But we don't want you to bring them over. We want to come over and pick 'em, pick the cows." So my husband went over and picked the cows then.

When we found out we could get them, he went over and picked the cows and brought them home. Jerseys and Guernseys. So they were all milking, a bucketful. We didn't have no place to put the milk, and we didn't have any customers. So the cows were all there, and so we had to throw the milk on the ground after we milked them.

We had the inspector come over to see if we could get a license, and he said he couldn't give us a license exceptin' we painted the buildings inside and out. So I told my husband to go to Seattle and look him up an old man for helping, and we cleaned the place up and lime-washed the barn inside and out So the inspector came over and he said, "This is more like it. This is the cleanest dairy I've seen now." So he gave us a license. So we started then.

144

And this little old man that came to work for us, Mr. Luther, said, "I'll go out on the route if nobody else will go, and get the customers."

And I said, "Can you sell milk?"

And he said, "Well, I should hope to tell the world. If I can sell suits for the International Tailoring Company for thirty years, I can sure sell a quart of milk with a half a pint of cream on it for ten cents."

So my husband took him on the route with him, and they each solicited customers, and he got twenty to my husband's ten every time. He told them that we'd been at the Country Club—this man was a pretty good talker—and we sold the milk that way. And this man stayed with us.

'Course our boys were going to school by that time, see. Junior was nine and John was thirteen or fourteen. So after they come home from school, they'd always help with the dairy work, and they were proud to be in the dairy—that was something. They would help feed the calves and whatever we had.

Well, we got some pigs to drink up the milk that we had to throw on the ground. And then the pigs got to be ready to butcher. We couldn't find anyone to butcher the pigs, so we finally found some Filipinos. Mr. Oreiro said, "Well, I'll see that the pigs get butchered. I'll come along and butcher them."

Well, I said, "You'll have to collect your own wood out of the woods and build your fire," and so he did. And then he poured boiling water over the pigs with a coffee can or something like that, and scraped each carcass. And then they cut up the meat all up, and they was taking the meat home as fast as they could. We weren't going to get any.

I finally went outside and I said, "You know my husband's going to be quite angry if he comes home and don't get any of that meat. You'll have to save him that other pig, or half of it at least." We didn't have any refrigeration then, you know. He had to buy ice. So anyway, they let us have the half of the pig. But they got the other pigs out of the way, so we didn't have to buy feed for them. And so, that was that for then.

Then we went on with six cows until we didn't have enough milk from the six cows to supply all the customers, because we kept gettin' new customers. They told each other all along what wonderful milk we had, so we had to buy more cows and more cows till we had thirty-five cows. We had to buy them on time. We didn't have enough money to pay cash for them. They were about one hundred dollars apiece, and so.

Then the hay. We had to buy hay too, and the hay was pretty high right then. So the man came along with the stuff to pick up the hay, because the cows wouldn't eat the hay. He'd brought us in some bad hay, and the cows wouldn't eat it. And he said, "They oughta eat that hay."

And I said, "Well, there's a cow that we bought from your father. She'll eat most anything. So let's give her some of the hay and see if she'll eat it." And she didn't. She turned her nose up at it. She wouldn't eat it, either.

But there was a trick to that, see. She was in heat so she wasn't eating, and I didn't tell him that and the man didn't know it. So that's why she wouldn't eat. So he took all the hay away, and I told him we was just youngsters startin' in. So he took all the hay away and brought us some decent loads of hay then. So we didn't have to pay any more for it, but they'd got it from a valley somewhere where there was a sewerage running through, and the cows can smell when the hay goes through where there's a sewerage, and they could smell the hay so they wouldn't eat it. Our cows wouldn't eat it.

So anyway, then, the next trouble we had, the well went dry. Then, with a horse and sleds we had to haul water out of the neighbor's well. There wasn't enough land—we had nine acres to start with, so we had to rent some in addition to that, some of the neighbors' land around that, so we could see if we could get our business going. And then when we got it going, why we couldn't stop then because everyone kept wanting more and more milk and more things.

Then that first man we rented from was very annoyed because we was goin' to move, but we knew we couldn't stay there with no water, couldn't run a dairy with no water. We had to slide it around and that's all we had. We had to haul water out of the neighbor's well and put it in our well.

And then someone came and offered us a ninety-six-acre farm where there was plenty of water. But it all had to be pioneered. There wasn't any electric light or anything.

And we came to look at that, and we looked it all over, and we knew we had a hard job to build a new barn, even though we could only rent it. So we built a new barn and a milk room and fixed the water situation so that we could put down into the crick where we could get water from. And so we had enough water for the cattle and plenty for the house.

Andrew Johnson rented us that. And he was ninety-six years old. They didn't think he would have very long to live so after he was gone they was going to sell us the farm. But while he was alive, he didn't want the farm sold, or, in other words, they didn't want him to sell.

So about inside of five years we paid twenty-two fifty a month rent for the ninety-six acres and the old house. There was no electricity. We had to get an easement from someone and put the electric light in, so we had electric light to milk with and to fix the barn. So it took us a month before we could move into that.

We finally got the electricity fixed at the new place, and we moved onto the Andrew Johnson farm then. We drove the cows all over from New Brooklyn Road to the Port Madison-Manzanita cutoff. That's where the place was. We'd been filling up the water for them to drink from the neighbor's well.

'Course there was a lot of ditching to be done, and fencing to be done, and everything that way, but we still was able to get some help, so we got eventually all done. Then we had to have seventy-five cows in order to supply the demand for milk. So we kept buyin' more and more cows, and adding them to what we had already.

We had just one man and our two selves and my son, and the little one. Leo was able to help a little bit then. He was nine years old. He was able to help quite a little bit. Said he could milk five cows if his dad would let him. So anyway, they had the milking machines then, so.

But you see, the boys was still goin' to school, so when they come home, they always helped and fed the cows, and put new

The Lovgreen dairy barn on Bainbridge Island, WA

hay to the calves and stuff like that. And the oldest one was milking some then, so I milked I don't know how many with the milking machine–about half of them anyway.

And so we went on with this until each year we had to pay two dollars more rent. Each year it went up a little bit, the rent. But that was goin' to stay at that. So then the Old Mister, Mr. Johnson, died, They was ready to sell the farm then in six months.

So they asked us if we'd like to buy the farm, and we said, yes, we would if the price was reasonable. Well, they wanted to charge us for all the ditching that we'd done and all the stuff there again, so we said we wasn't goin' to pay for all that. It was agreed that we didn't have to pay for anything that we'd worked and done on the place. We couldn't do that. We couldn't pay for that work over again.

Minnie Rose Lovgreen

So he said they wanted quite a bit for the property, and we would move rather than pay them more than the place was worth. So we found another place, and we told them that we had another place to go to. He said that it would cost us money to move. And we said it wouldn't cost us any more to move, because we could drive the cows where they had to go like we drove them over there.

So I said, "All right then. If you don't want to come down in the price, then we'll just plan on moving."

And then he was just ready to hang up, and I said, "There's just one more last thought, now. If you sell the place to someone else, what will they have to make their living on? Because they can't have another dairy–there's already too many dairies. And it isn't a place for growing strawberries. It's too much wet land." And so on, and so on.

I said, "What will they have to make a living on so they can pay you, make the payments to you?" And he said he hadn't thought of that, so he gave in and let us have the place at the price that we agreed on. I think it was ten thousand dollars. That was real reasonable then.

Then we came a lot of times and looked over their things, and there was some people living in the little house where their father had lived, and they was supposed to move, soon as the father passed away, soon as we took over the place, but they didn't want to move. So when they didn't want to move, then they complained because our horse was getting in their pasture there by the house and their clothes was on the line, and they said it made flies go on their clothesline. So we decided that, in the agreement that we had, that they were supposed to move soon as the father died, so we told him that, and so they had to move then.

So then we had the place all to ourselves. We was glad that they had to move, because they were disagreeable anyway, and they were drinking a lot.

We bought ice from a Mr. Johnson, the auto freight man. He had a big ice house. We had to go and get it in the night. We had an icebox, you know, to keep ice in. It was all insulated. We put that ice over the top of the milk bottles and that kept the milk cold till the milk got delivered. 'Course in the wintertime we didn't have to do that.

Milking time at the Lovgreen's prize-winning dairy

And then after I'd fed the hired men their breakfast, and the ones that was goin' to school got off to school, I went right out and helped them to do the barn work and clean up out there,

151

get all ready for the inspector. We washed the milking parlors down, and washed the barn, you know, where it had to be hosed down, and put sawdust on the floors so the cows wouldn't slip down, and then lime over that, to make it sanitary. That was a deodorizer. It wouldn't smell then a'tall, a beautiful, clean barn. They said they could eat off of our floor, it was so clean. And then we'd sweep the mangers where the cows eat out of.

And they had drinking cups and we had to clean out the drinking bowls so that when they come in they knew enough to press on the lever to help themselves to water. There's a little lever in the bottom of the drinking bowls, so that when they come in they knew enough to press on the lever to help themselves to water. They'd press on that with their nose and bring the water up, so they got water that way. They soon learned how to do that.

And of course when we had new calves, why someone had to look after them. There was always something. So I'd work out there until about ten o'clock in the morning and then the barn work was all done, nine thirty or ten, and then I could go in the house and clean up the house, and get ready to cook dinner and wash clothes or whatever we had to do.

And then call the hired men in to lunch. They wanted a big dinner in the middle of the day as well as at night. Lamb stew or beef stew or somepin' like that, you know–and potatoes and mashed potatoes and all those sort of things. And then some kind of dessert—either rice pudding or milk pudding of some kind, or custards. Otherwise some kind of cake or biscuits, cookies, So we had all that.

After they had their lunch they could take an hour's rest, an hour or two's rest, and then by the time the bottles come home, why they had to help unload the truck and then get all ready with me to help to wash bottles.

My husband came home, and then if he didn't have all his lunch with him, then he got some more when he got home and then he went upstairs and slept for an hour. And then he went out to milk again at three o'clock, the same as he would early in the morning. So that was that. And then after all the bottles was done, then they'd start milking the cows and then my son would start filling all the bottles for the next morning.

We had quite a refrigerating room there. Everything was going fast. We could keep ice and everything in there. There was some wire, like chicken wire, and a lot of insulation, and a concrete floor. So it was all concrete walls, and they could hose them down, you know. They had a real heavy door that you'd shut, and that would keep the cold in.

They had a bucket that hangs on the cows. They had belts that went over their backs, and then they hung the bucket on the belt underneath their stomachs, and they milked right into the pail. And then they'd take and empty that overflow into a cooler. The cooler water run through the hollows of it and milk run over the outside of it, and that cooled the milk off to a certain temperature. They used the milk cans whenever they had too much milk left over.

They'd put it in the milk cans then and ship it or, you know, let it go to Carnation or Christopherson, or whoever was in the market for buying milk. We didn't usually have too much left over. Then, when they come back from the route, and if they had too much milk left, well sometimes we used that for the calves. That was   all whole milk, rich.   And so we could fill the bottles again. My son could fill the bottles by hand.

There was a milk tank there, and it had a faucet on it, a great big milk tank with a faucet on it. He'd hold the bottles under the faucet and fill them that way, and then put the cap on. The cap had to be put on straight. If it wasn't on straight, well you got a grade less for your milk.

You had to order so many thousand, you know, when you ordered the caps. They come in rolls, so you had to order so many in order to get your supply in. We used a lot of caps. They came already printed up. We had to order them from the dairy machinery or from the factory, and they had your name on it and the telephone number, and everything.

You always had to be ready to give the hired men their money and let 'em go and hire somebody else, hurry up and phone up and hire somebody else. It wasn't always easy to get someone. You had to be real nice to them. If you weren't nice to them, they'd tell them in the employment office that you didn't give them good food or somepin' like that, you know, so you had to be real nice to them in order to keep them there, tell them that if there was an opportunity sometime we'd take them back again, if we were firing them.

Sometimes we had to fire them if they weren't good, if they weren't good milkers. Some of them only had 3 fingers on 1 hand, and they couldn't milk with only three fingers on one hand. They'd lost their fingers somehow, so we couldn't have them to milk that way. They'd ruin the cows.

We changed men every two, three, or four months. Often times it was they wanted to go, sometimes it was us wanted to get rid of them. It'd depend on how disagreeable they were, you know, or how they were.

The Lovgreen home at the dairy

**The Lovgreens gave tours to school groups
and received many thank-you notes.**

Minnie Rose Lovgreen

And then we had a polite way of lettin' 'em go. Always told them, called them in and didn't give 'em any notice a'tall, told them to get their things ready because we're going to let them go back to town on that boat. And so, give 'em an extra dollar or so, somepin' like that, for the boat fare.

They were glad to go, some of 'em was glad to go, specially if they were the kind that liked to celebrate a little bit and wandered off. Some of 'em would only work just about a month and then they wanted to go, anyway. They had a month's pay coming to them, and that was quite a little bit when the wages went out.

We had one man that stayed, I think, a couple of years or more. We got him through the employment office. He was a German fellow, and he was pretty good. And then we had to let him go. I don't know why my husband decided to let him go. I think it was because he went visiting next door too much.

Oh yes. We won the trophy twice for having the highest-testing milk. We would have won the trophy a third time, and then if we won it the third time we'd get to keep the trophy, except that the cap on the bottle wasn't quite straight and that was the only thing that disqualified us. We got ninety-six points, I think.

But the inspector when he come to our place would drink a whole quart of milk. He was a good milk drinker. He said it was the best milk out. He wasn't afraid of getting fat either. He was plenty fat, but wasn't afraid of getting any fatter. Some of our men would drink quite a lot of milk at their mealtime. They could have all have they wanted. There was one cow we had. I think they took a picture. She took first prize for giving the highest-testing milk and the most milk. She was Guernsey and Brown Swiss. She was more of a brindle. She was very pretty–the one in the strawberry booklet. There was another one in that photograph that was her mother, we kept the daughter. We always kept the daughter of the good cows.

We could do most anything with our cows because they were easy to take care of. We didn't let the men handle them rough. My husband was very gentle with the cows. He had a little rag that he used to wash off their udders with, and he'd just give them a little pat with the rag, you know, and tell them to get over and they'd get over so he could start putting the machines on them.

In the evening, why they all went to milking about three o'clock or three-thirty, and then they got in the house around six thirty at night and I'd have a big dinner for them. Well, there was always meat and potatoes. See sometimes at lunchtime, if I cooked enough, it could be warmed over, potatoes fried and stuff like that. But in the evening, then you had to have a new batch of everything. And then fruit or somepin' like that for dessert—fruit and cake. If you served fruit, you always had to have cake or cookies with it. But they always had plenty to eat.

We had a big vegetable garden, too. We worked that in between acts. It was about a quarter of an acre or so. We grew beans and tomatoes and turnips and carrots–we grew a lot of carrots. Potatoes and raspberries too. We'd pick our raspberries and then have raspberries for dessert. It was real good.

And then, of course, we had quite an apple orchard then too, you know. We used to have to do them trees in between acts, prune the trees and look after them. We had real large apples like the twenty-ounce Pippins and Jonathans, I think.

And then we had another little apple called a russet. I haven't seen any russets around, but we used to have a little tree called a russet. We like that very much. I'd like to get a russet apple tree. We'd plant it somewhere around here where it would grow, somewhere just down below there, I think, or plant it right out here near the gate, you know, inside the gate there where the others are.

**The Lovgreen family: Minnie Rose,
John, Leo, Jr., and husband Leo**

Note

Here ends Minnie Rose's story of those, busy early years with their highly successful Bainbridge Dairy on Bainbridge Island, Washington. In 1975, she did describe the rest of those dairy years while dictating this life story into my tape recorder. But unfortunately, as we were transcribing her story later that year, that particular tape disappeared–much to our regret.

Minnie Rose, however, with her usual upbeat attitude, would have said that if one tape had to be lost that was the best choice—because by that time her lifetime of "always looking ahead" had born sweet fruit—russets and otherwise. And she would have loved seeing this next chapter as the end of her life story.

Nancy Rekow
May, 2010

Chapter Six

1955....

Visit to England~Return Home

~ "It was wonderful to go bashin' around
in a strange country all alone."
~ "She didn't see how I could have come all that way and
found the place and everything, and grown up
like that, all this time, see, 55 years."

One day in September in 1955, I was finishing my lunch and the phone rang and it was Art Linkletter from California. He said, "Would you like to earn some money?"

I said, "Oh yes."

Then he said, "The old woman who lived in the shoe, what did she feed her children on? You have three minutes to answer the question."

And I said, "She gave them some broth without any bread."

He said, "Good, you have earned fifty-five dollars." That was a start, as my husband and son said I should go to England and see my sisters I had not seen in fifty-five years. So I got ready and they took me to the airport, put me on the plane. I went for three weeks.

That was the first time I'd ever been on a plane. And when it landed in New York at eight o'clock in the morning, and I had to set in New York all day waitin' for the plane to go on to England. And so I wrote letters all the time I was setting there. The time went fast when I was writing.

**Minnie Rose chats with Becky and Mitch,
two of Nancy Rekow's children.**

Then we went to a place called Gander, and we went there. And I didn't know whether we had to change planes there, but it seems like we stopped there for something. And then we went on to Manchester. And they were serving free coffee with brandy in it.

And I met a lady on the plane that had a little child, and I helped her with that, while she would go to the washroom to get her hair done, and so on. Then I took care of the baby while she was doing that. Then we got off at at another place in

London. Then we thought we would get ourselves some coffee and a little lunch there.

And there was one waitress there at tables, where it had all been full and they were messy, they were short of help. So I asked if they would give us a napkin, and the waitress didn't know what a napkin was. She thought it meant a baby's diaper, and she looked at me and said, "We don't have any."

And then I thought for a minute and I said, "Well, serviette." So then she knew what I meant. I wanted to wipe the table off. And the baby was about nine or ten months old, so she was spitting up a little bit, so we did need some help.

So after we had somepin' to eat she changed her baby into a clean dress and that. She was goin' to have her mother meet her there, so that was the end of us and we didn't see each other anymore. We thought we'd see each other after we got going home or somepin' like that, but we didn't. I think she wrote to me and I didn't write back.

Anyway then we went and looked after our baggage to go to another part of London, I think it was, to London—this must have been Manchester we was at–to London, and they had to load up suitcases to go to Wisbech (Cambridgeshire). I wanted to go to Wisbech from there. So I went to the different stations to find out how the trains went, and I didn't have any luck for quite a while, then finally I did.

But I couldn't get my second suitcase, so I told the man I had another suitcase, and he couldn't find it, and he said you wait for a while, wait a while till all the others have gone, and then we'll find it. So the others had all gone, but the other suitcase didn't show up. So I told him that I had to have it. I said there was no use to travel, going someplace, and not have your things. And I said the suitcase wasn't locked, it was done up with a strap, strapped up.

So he said he couldn't find it, it wasn't there, it hadn't come, and I said, "Well, that's too bad. Well, I'll have to give you my address where I'm going, and when you get it, it'll have to be forwarded to me, because it's important that I get it. I won't be there very long, so you would need to mail it right away."

**Minnie Rose (back right), Nancy Rekow (holding son)
and assorted friends**

I said, "Don't you have an arrangement where you can telephone and ask what happened to it?" I said, "We do. We can get on the phone and find out what happened to a suitcase in a short while in America."

So he said, "Well we'll look out for it," so I know he didn't like that too well.

"Well," I said, "don't you have such things?"

And he said, "No."

So I asked someone else about the suitcase, and they said, "Well, did you ask the porter?"—that was one of the boys there.

"Yes, I did."

"Well, I wonder if he knew anything about it. He shouldn't have a uniform on unless he knew his business."

And so anyway they were kind of afraid and they hunted me up the suitcase. They got the suitcase and sent it along. And when I got to Wisbech it came. They shipped it on.

'Course the roads and everything was better, and there was better streets and that than when I was there. But otherways their language, their accents was all about the same. You had to listen to hear what they were talking about. Sometimes they talked so quick that you didn't catch on to what they were talkin' about.

But my sisters did not know me.

When I got to Wisbech, then I think I took a taxi up to where my sister was supposed to live, and she wasn't home, there was nobody home. I had mailed them a letter, but there was nobody home.

So I walked a little way up the street and I saw two little boys, and they were loading up, shoveling up gravel in a little red wagon, I asked them if they would show me where Mrs. uh

Nancy with Elizabeth Hutchison Zwick, illustrator of *Minnie Rose Lovgreen's Recipe for Raising Chickens* (with daughter Hanya)

uh what's her name now, where Mrs. Ward lived–that was my sister's daughter, married daughter.

One of them–they kept on shoveling away like they didn't want to pay any attention–and the one little boy said, "Oh come on, help her you dope." So I told them I'd give 'em a penny. And so they walked a little way up the street with me and showed me where Princess Street was.

And I knocked on a door there, and I thought surely that would be the place. And the lady opened the door about three inches and peeked out, and I said, "Does Mrs. Ward live here?

"No, oh no, there's no one here that name."

"Well, they told me that she lived on this street. This is Princess Street."

"Oh," she said, "you must go further up the street there and there's a large bay window. Remember the bay window, that's where she lives. It sticks out. Don't forget the bay window."

Well, I couldn't remember at first what a bay window looked like. And then I used to hear them say that when a man was fat that he had a big bay window. So I thought, well, it'll be a window that sticks out. So I went up to that bay window, and I knocked on the door, and my niece came to the door, and so I asked her if Mrs. Ward lived there, if she was Mrs. Ward, and she said yes she was, she was Mrs. Ward. But she acted frightened, too. They all acted frightened about opening their doors.

So I said then, "Uh, if you are Mrs. Ward, then I must be your Aunt Minnie."

So my sister was right behind her, and my sister put her hand up on her chest, and she said, "Oh no, that can't be you. That can't be you." She'd hadn't seen me since I was about ten years old.

And so I said "Yes,"that was it."

"How did you come?"

"I came by plane."

So anyway, they asked me in, so I went in. She didn't see how I could have come all that way and found the place and everything, and grown up like that, all this time, see, fifty-five years. So when she studied me quite a little bit, she said I looked like my oldest brother, one of the older brothers. So that was that. So we visited and we had tea.

And they told me I would have to stay there all night, because my sister didn't have enough room in her house for me. So Edna said, Mrs. Ward said, it was all right for me to stay there all night. So they, after we talked for a while and that, then it was time for me to go to bed, and they got me to bed.

And I didn't sleep hardly all night, I just couldn't sleep. I don't know whether it was the plane or what it was, but I just couldn't sleep, so in the morning I said I hardly slept a wink.

Minnie Rose Lovgreen with Nancy Rekow at the book-signing party for *Recipe for Raising Chickens* in May, 1975, two months before she died.

She said ,"Yes, I knew you tossed and turned all night."

"Do you have any aspirins?"

"Well, I have something different than aspirins. I have Dispirins. That'll put you to sleep."so she gave me one Dispirin

Minnie Rose Lovgreen

and something to drink it down with.

I don't know how I ever made it alone. It was wonderful to go bashin' around in a strange country all alone, especially through London. You had to ask this, ask that. I could no more do it now than flying.

So anyway, I slept then. And I slept and I slept. And then they couldn't wake me up when they wanted to wake me up. So my sister and my niece stood. And they were so afraid that I was knocked out altogether, that I'd never wake up again. They was always afraid, yeah, they was terribly afraid. And I didn't know whether they was afraid they'd have me on their hands or what. But anyway they was afraid.

So after I got up, then we had some tea for breakfast, and fruit and stuff. Then I felt better and we walked around, we visited there.

Then my sister told me, she said, "I had a letter from our other sister, Georgiana, and she said, 'I shan't pay any more attention to when she writes and says she's comin', because she'll never come.'" And there I was, see, when the letter came.

In the letter Georgiana said, "I'm goin' to send that right back to her. She'll never come. She keeps on sayin' she was coming and then she'll never come."

Well, I was goin' to go to England three weeks before that, but my brother died, he died in his sleep. And I would have gone, but he died in his sleep, see, so that was that. And we woulda had a wonderful time together. He was the one (brother) that was always so attentive to the things around home, the one that went to Peterborough to make the bricks.

So anyway, then that held us up. I had to go home to his funeral, and that held me up for another three week, you see. I think then I had written to say that I was coming later, I'd be there, but then I got there before the letter did. They hadn't gotten the letter.

They were real happy to see me, but they didn't ask, and I thought they'd ask, I thought they'd ask a lot of questions about America, but they didn't ask any questions, so there really wasn't a great deal to talk about. And they don't seem to want to talk about their things very much. In other words, they think they shouldn't brag. They think we brag and they don't.

So anyhow, I went to visit that other sister then, because they couldn't phone each other, didn't have house phones. So we wrote and told her that we was there and we was coming, and she wrote right back and said for me to go and put in a week over there when I had gotten finished with Wisbech. So we did, we drove over, and we had tea with them. And then my sister rode back.

They charged, I think it was fourteen shillings each to take us there in the taxicab–fourteen shillings each. And then after I got home my sister wrote and said the man made a mistake, it should've been more. So I said, if he made a mistake and it should've been more it's his own lookout. I'm not goin' to pay any more.

I thought he'd figured I was from America, because they always said that—"Don't let them know that she's from America–don't let her go in that bank alone because they'll rob her." They said, "They know you're American," or, "Don't let her pay for the lunch that we were goin' to have out, because they'll know she's American. They'll soak her."So that was the way it was.

Then we had a week with the other sister, and we visited the old farm where we used to live, you know, and the old farmhouse and everything, and they had homemade bread coming out of the big brick oven, which was real nice. And butter—homemade churned butter. It tasted so good.

Some cousins of mine were living there—Horace and Gloria Harrison–so they had this bread comin' out of the oven and they were real nice and showed us all over the house and everything, you know. So it was very much the same.

They had tore down a little part of the boys' bedrooms, I think, and just had one upstairs way there,

And they did–I don't know what they'd done—something with the dairy, I think, or the pantry. I can't remember just what that was.

I went from there then to Derbyshire to visit my other sister. So I visited with her, and she wasn't hardly able to walk around, she was kinda' crippled up with arthritis. So I visited there for a while with her and her husband. And then I decided to go to Croyden and visit my nephew that pilots the airplane for BOAC. So I went there and stayed there all night.

And then, the day I was 'sposed to come home, we went to the airport, and they said they didn't have any reservations for me. They had forgotten to phone in the reservations, make note of the reservations for coming back. So anyway, my nephew then brought me back, and I had to stay at his place another couple of days until there was a reservation.

But anyway, then when we went to the airplane the next time, why there was the reservations right there, because my nephew phoned up and made all the arrangements.

We had to go up the escalator, and I can't ride the escalator. I never could ride the escalator. So he and my sister went up the escalator, and when they looked behind I was still standing down at the bottom, and there wasn't too much time for the plane. So my nephew beckoned for me to come on up, and I told him, I shook my head, I couldn't come up. So he had to come down another way, and come and get hold of me and take me up. So I got up there anyway.

And then we got a cup of tea or something just to pass the time away, till we got on the plane. Then there wasn't any more changing. So that was the comin' home. When I got into Seattle there was a different atmosphere altogether. The American people had such a way of smiling at you, welcoming you, and anyway I felt a whole lot better when I got back in my own country again. There wasn't that suspicion that you had to be afraid of this and afraid of that.

And then when I came home, there were some more people that shared the cab with me to the ferry dock. We were landed in the morning. So I got home about nine o'clock in the morning. And the farm folks were just finishing their breakfast. And they were surprised when they saw me come up in a taxi. I said I was tired. They was really surprised to see me get home that fast, you know. I got back home (to Bainbridge Island) about nine o'clock in the morning. But there was one little bag that I had when I was coming in the taxi, and somehow it got

Minnie Rose Lovgreen

left in the taxi when I got out to go and run for the ferry. Then someone came running up to the ferry with a little bag for me.

And I just thought, well, what a wonderful country this was.

Minnie Rose Lovgreen, age 24, in 1912

Afterword

For Elizabeth, the illustrator, and for me, putting together that first book, *Minnie Rose Lovgreen's Recipe for Raising Chickens*, was a labor of love for our friend who was dying. With six young children between us, we accomplished things we'd never otherwise have attempted.

In the years that followed, Elizabeth became a graphic designer, a fine painter, and continued to illustrate books. I published poems, taught poetry and creative writing to all ages, and worked as an editor. Over the years, Elizabeth and I have collaborated on other books and projects. But we both know it all started with Minnie Rose Lovgreen.

* * *

My partner Everett Thompson, a retired English teacher who never knew Minnie Rose, has helped every step of the way to publish this book. I could never have done it without him. Thank you, Everett.

Nancy Rekow
June, 2010

Acknowledgements

Without the help and patience of many people, this book would not exist. Thank you to the many understanding friends, experts, and professionals who answered questions, read and commented on the manuscript, and wrote comments and blurbs–and to John and Duncan Newland-Thompson, who must have wondered if we had been chained to our computers.

These names constitute, at best, a partial list of those who have helped.

Kathleen Alcala, Rachel Bauch, Book Publishers Northwest, Linda Carlson, Gerry Elfendahl, Andy Enefer, Cynthia Frank, Sandy Gould, Pam Griffin, Scott Harris, Hank Helm, Patricia Hill,

Independent Book Publishers Association, Rebecca Judd, Paul Krupin, Betsy Leger, Trudy Lisagor, Ann Lovejoy, Bob McAllister, Connie Mears, Jacob Meier, Lynn Mitchell

Justin Nodolf, Pacific Northwest Booksellers Association, Nicole Ratana, Bob Royce, Staff at Eagle Harbor Book Co., Kathleen Thorne, Beverley West, Elizabeth Hutchison Zwick

Most of all, we remember Minnie Rose Lovgreen who, sick and in the hospital, poured her lively and detailed memories into Nancy Rekow's tape recorder those many years ago.

Far As I Can Remember

Minnie Rose Lovgreen
1888-1975

She skipped lunch to work
   the garden.
Spring had been late.
Poppies had self-seeded
   through lettuce.
She tied up the pole beans
with saved twine, wilted
weeds in piles
to be dug in.

Fingers crusted, she worked
till the sun was butter
   churning,
roses funneled wild from all
   gardens known,
and she crumpled like a
   burlap sack.
Sunstroke, she thought. But
sun had nothing to do
with the flowering in her
   blood.

After the funeral
we are all

invited to tea
at her house.
It is a fine day.
The sky is blue.
Not a cloud.

On our laps
the teacups pose. Geraniums
scream from the flowerpots.
Outside, in late sun,
chickens take dust baths.
Already the gravensteins
hang in tight green knots.

Old woman,
I brought you roses and baby's
   breath
in a mason jar
one week before you died.
Past the oxygen tubes
you tried to tell me again
they had been your bridal
   bouquet.

~Nancy Rekow

To order

Far As I Can Remember: An Immigrant Woman's Story, 1888-1975
by Minnie Rose Lovgreen
or
Minnie Rose Lovgreen's Recipe for Raising Chickens

go to:

nwtrilliumpress.com
buyolympia.com
your local independent bookstore
amazon.com

or phone

NW Trillium Press
(206) 842-6908

or write to us at

NW Trillium Press
5591 Battle Point Drive NE
Bainbridge Island, WA 98110